BLAST FROM THE *PAST*

BLAST FROM THE PAST

Warning: Small parts may be a choking hazard. Not for children under 3 years.

ACKNOWLEDGEMENTS

A big thanks to all those who worked so hard (and so fast!) on this project . . .
Writing/research team: Erin Conley, Lani Stackel, Maria Llull,
Katie Ranftle, and Bob Moog
Editing team: Erin Conley, Heather Russell-Revesz, and Bob Moog
Proofing/fact-checking team: Heather Russell-Revesz, Rick Campbell,
Suzanne Cracraft, and Amanda Banks
Design/production team: Jeff Batzli, Richela Morgan, and Michael Friedman
Sales and promotions team: Jules Herbert, Bruce Lubin, Mary Carlomagno,
and Michael Friedman
We couldn't have done it without you!

Design: Lindgren/Fuller Design

Copyright © 2004 by Spinner Books

ISBN 1-57528-909-1

Printed in China

04 05 MP 9 8 7 6 5 4 3

CONTENTS

RULES

For 1 or more players!

OBJECT
Put on your pop culture cap, blast to the past, and be the first player to earn 15 points!

CATEGORIES
Fact or Phooey?: Tell which statements are fact and which are phooey.
Hot or Not?: Put on your hot pants and guess which fads were hot and which fads were *not*!
Rapid Recall: Test your trivia know-how through the decades.
Order Up!: Put pivotal events in the order they happened from earliest to latest.
Hit Parade: Think vinyl. Think eight-track. Now, get ready to sing some old favorites.
Dead or Alive?: Guess who was still talking and who was done walking within the given decade.

THE WAY TO PLAY
First things first: grab a pen and paper to keep track of your points.

The youngest player is the **Reader** for the first round and may not play until the second round. The **Reader** spins to determine the decade (i.e. '60s, '70s, '80s, or '90s) and reads the first question from that section to the player on his/her left.

If the player guesses correctly, s/he receives a point for that topic and play continues in a clockwise direction.

If the player guesses incorrectly, play continues in a clockwise direction. There is no penalty for an incorrect response.

Play continues in a clockwise direction with the **Reader** reading the next player a question from the next category in the block until *all questions on the page* have been asked.

(For example, if there are three players, the first player gets **Fact or Phooey?**, the second player gets **Hot or Not?**, the third gets **Rapid Recall**. Then, the first player gets **Order Up!** and so on … Got it? Good!).

Don't worry if one player gets the opportunity to answer more than one question—the advantage will shift with each spin!

After all players have answered a question, the person to the **Reader's** left takes a spin and is now the **Reader** for the next block of questions.

WINNING THE GAME
The first player to collect 15 points is the winner!

PLAYING ON YOUR OWN
Spin, flip to the first page of the round, and read the topic question from the appropriate section. Don't forget to keep the answer covered with a bookmark!

If you guess correctly, give yourself a point and spin again. If you guess incorrectly, take away a point. If you have no points, simply continue playing.

Collect 20 points in twenty minutes or less and you're a winner!

1960s

BLAST FROM THE *PAST*

1

FACT OR PHOOEY? Natalie Wood recorded all her own vocals in *West Side Story*.
Phooey! Wood lip-synched to singer Marni Nixon's voice.

HOT OR NOT? Ouiji Boards
Hot. In the late 1960s, Americans went wacky for Ouiji, and squandered millions on the spooky boards.

RAPID RECALL **Q:** First-time novelist Harper Lee topped the bestseller lists and took home the 1961 Pulitzer Prize for what classic story featuring a girl named Scout?
A: *To Kill a Mockingbird*

ORDER UP! **A.** Howdy Doody hangs up his hat after 13 years on the air.
B. Neil Armstrong takes "one giant leap for mankind" in his historic walk on the moon.
A. (1960) B. (1967)

HIT PARADE **Q:** Fill in the blank in this Mamas and Papas' hit: "I've been for a walk on a winter's day. I'd be safe and warm if I was __ ___."
A: in L.A. (from "California Dreamin' ")

DEAD OR ALIVE? Gypsy Rose Lee
Alive. Lee's bawdy burlesque made her a star, and kept her kicking until her death in 1970.

BLAST FROM THE PAST

2

FACT OR PHOOEY? Janet Leigh's character steals $40,000 from her work, just prior to being murdered in *Psycho*.
Fact. Apparently, crime really doesn't pay!

HOT OR NOT? Chatty Cathy
Hot. This charming little chatterbox debuted in 1959, and remained a must-have item for girls throughout the '60s.

RAPID RECALL **Q:** What boy faces his fears in Maurice Sendak's *Where the Wild Things Are*, first published in 1963?
A: Max

ORDER UP! **A.** Richard M. Nixon is sworn in as 37th President of the United States.
B. The Jimi Hendrix Experience plays at the Monterey Pop Festival.
B. (1967) A. (1969)

HIT PARADE **Q:** If you take the last train to Clarksville, what band will meet you at the station?
A: The Monkees (from "Last Train to Clarksville")

DEAD OR ALIVE? Jackie Robinson
Alive. Baseball's great didn't strike out till 1972.

BLAST FROM THE *PAST*

3

FACT OR PHOOEY? Alfred Hitchcock's classic *The Birds* is set in California.
Fact. It mostly takes place in San Francisco and Bodega Bay.

HOT OR NOT? *The Rocky Horror Picture Show*
Not. This funky flick made midnight moviegoing a phenomenon, but it didn't become a cult classic until its big screen debut in the mid-'70s.

RAPID RECALL **Q:** What 12-inch action figure first took the toy market by storm in 1964?
A: G.I. Joe

ORDER UP! **A.** A House of Representatives committee holds "payola" hearings; *American Bandstand*'s Dick Clark denies involvement in the scandal.
B. Allen Ginsberg coins the phrase "flower power" to describe his non-violent strategy of political action.
A. (1960) B. (1965)

HIT PARADE **Q:** Fill in the blanks from this 1966 hit: "Now, what becomes of the _____ _____, who had love that's now departed?"
A: broken hearted (from Jimmy Ruffin's "What Becomes of the Broken Hearted")

DEAD OR ALIVE? Albert Einstein
Dead. The German-born genius who brought us relativity died in his sleep in 1955.

BLAST FROM THE PAST

4

FACT OR PHOOEY? *The Graduate* features a young woman who has an affair with an older, married man.
Phooey! The complete reverse, actually: a young man has an affair with an older, wedded woman (and then falls for her daughter!).

HOT OR NOT? Fallout shelters
Hot. The popularity of these underground homes away from home peaked as the Cuban Missile Crisis loomed in the early '60s.

RAPID RECALL **Q:** In 1968, furniture designer Charles Prior introduced what type of mattress after experimenting with Jell-O® and cornstarch?
A: The waterbed

ORDER UP! **A.** The U.S. eats Russian space dust after cosmonaut Yuri Gagarin becomes the first man to orbit Earth.
B. The first *Star Trek* episode, "The Man Trap," premieres. The storyline features a creature that sucks salt from human bodies.
A. (1961) B. (1966)

HIT PARADE **Sing** a line from the 1962 hit "The Monster Mash." (Don't know it? Make it up!)

DEAD OR ALIVE? Billie Burke (a.k.a. *The Wizard of Oz*'s Glinda)
Alive. The Good Witch of the North met her grave in 1970.

BLAST FROM **THE PAST**

5

FACT OR PHOOEY? Dennis Hopper directed and co-starred in *Easy Rider*.
Fact.

HOT OR NOT? Poodle skirts
Not. The poofy poodle skirt didn't stand a chance once the mini made headlines in the early '60s.

RAPID RECALL **Q:** What was the more popular name for *Artemia nyos*, a seemingly magical underwater 1960s "toy"?
A: Sea Monkeys

ORDER UP! **A.** Stanley Kubrick's *2001: A Space Odyssey* takes off at the box office.
B. NBC viewers witness Dallas strip-club owner Jack Ruby shoot accused Kennedy assassin Lee Harvey Oswald.
B. (1963) A. (1968)

HIT PARADE **Q:** Where did "your love" keep on lifting Jackie Wilson in 1967?
A: Higher and higher

DEAD OR ALIVE? Billie Holiday
Dead. This lady sang the blues until she died in 1959.

6

FACT OR PHOOEY? *Midnight Cowboy* was the first X-rated movie to win an Oscar® for Best Picture.
Fact.

HOT OR NOT? Super Balls
Hot. Wham-O® released this little round idea in the summer of 1965. By Christmas of that year, Super Balls were selling in the millions.

RAPID RECALL **Q:** What 1960s phenomenon made white clothes, teeth, eyeballs, and sometimes secret messages glow in the dark?
A: The black light

ORDER UP! **A.** Jackie Kennedy weds Greek millionaire Aristotle Onassis.
B. Andy Warhol causes a stir in the art world with his Campbell's Soup Cans.
B. (1962) A. (1968)

HIT PARADE **Q:** In a 1969 Three Dog Night hit, what number is the loneliest number?
A: One

DEAD OR ALIVE? Buddy Holly
Dead. "Peggy Sue's" singer died in a tragic plane crash in 1959.

7

FACT OR PHOOEY? *G.I. Blues* is a Gene Kelly musical.
Phooey! It's an Elvis movie.

HOT OR NOT? *The Mike Douglas Show*
Hot. Mike Douglas was the toast of the talk show for nearly two decades starting in 1961.

RAPID RECALL **Q:** In 1961, what Yankee beat Babe Ruth's home run record?
A: Roger Maris

ORDER UP! **A.** Apollo 11 astronauts Neil Armstrong and Buzz Aldrin take their historic Moonwalk.
B. Widespread riots rock the Los Angeles South Central neighborhood of Watts.
B. (1965) A. (1969)

HIT PARADE **Q:** In 1964, where did The Drifters like to hang out when they were down by the sea?
A: Under the boardwalk

DEAD OR ALIVE? Vivian Vance (*I Love Lucy*'s Ethel Mertz)
Alive. Lucy's gal pal and neighbor didn't die until 1979.

BLAST FROM THE PAST

8

FACT OR PHOOEY? *101 Dalmatians* was 1961's highest-grossing movie, beating out *West Side Story.*
Fact.

HOT OR NOT? "Moon River"
Hot. This Henry Mancini classic hit the airwaves—and topped the charts—in the early 1960s.

RAPID RECALL Q: Which cartoon character, first seen on television screens in 1969, never uttered a word?
A: The Pink Panther

ORDER UP! **A.** *The Sound of Music* delights moviegoers, and is one of the top-grossing films of the year.
B. Kennedy and Nixon go tête-à-tête in the first televised presidential debate.
B. (1960) A. (1965)

HIT PARADE **Sing** a line from the Supremes "Stop! In the Name of Love."

DEAD OR ALIVE? George Orwell
Dead. *1984's* prolific—and prophetic—author died in 1950.

BLAST FROM THE PAST

9

FACT OR PHOOEY? *Yellow Submarine* was the first Beatles movie released in the U.S.
Phooey! Their first was *A Hard Day's Night* in 1966.

HOT OR NOT? Davy Crockett–style coonskin caps
Not. The cult of Crockett lasted just a year, after 40 million Americans watched Fess Parker portray Davy on the Walt Disney show in 1954.

RAPID RECALL **Q:** Polly Purebread was the girlfriend of what popular 1960s caped canine crusader?
A: Underdog

ORDER UP! **A.** Charles Manson's deranged "family" murders actress Sharon Tate and three others.
B. British bandits escape with close to $7 million in the Great Train Robbery.
B. (1963) A. (1969)

HIT PARADE **Q:** What band had a straightforward name and two hits in the late '60s with "The Weight" and "Up on Cripple Creek"?
A: The Band

DEAD OR ALIVE? Carmen Miranda
Dead. This dancer, famous for her fruit-laden hats, died in 1955.

10

FACT OR PHOOEY? *The Beverly Hillbillies* called their swimming pool an oil slick.
Phooey! The Clampetts called their pool a cement pond.

HOT OR NOT? The Baby Boom
Not. The Baby Boom occurred just after WWII, in 1944 and 1945, when GIs returned home and made babies.

RAPID RECALL **Q:** Who won the very first Super Bowl, held in 1967?
A: The Green Bay Packers defeated the Kansas City Chiefs, 35 – 10.

ORDER UP! **A.** *Shindig!* hits the airwaves.
B. Ken Kesey publishes *One Flew Over the Cuckoo's Nest.*
B. (1962) A. (1964)

HIT PARADE **Sing** a line from "The Lion Sleeps Tonight."

DEAD OR ALIVE? Charles A. Lindbergh
Alive. This Spirit of St. Louis pilot lived until 1974.

11

FACT OR PHOOEY? Introduced in 1967, Lite-Brite was a glow-in-the-dark doll.
Phooey! It was a versatile toy that allowed tots to make colorful mosaic pictures that lit up on a black screen.

HOT OR NOT? 3D movies
Not. The 3D movie craze peaked—and faded—in the early 1950s.

RAPID RECALL **Q:** Who lost the race for the White House to John F. Kennedy in 1960?
A: Richard M. Nixon

ORDER UP! **A.** President Johnson declares "war on poverty."
B. Betty Friedan's *The Feminine Mystique* gives the women's movement a groundbreaking boost.
B. (1963) A. (1964)

HIT PARADE **Sing** a line from the theme song to TV's *Gilligan's Island*.

DEAD OR ALIVE? Humphrey Bogart
Dead. Bogie kicked the bucket in 1957.

BLAST FROM THE PAST

12

FACT OR PHOOEY? In 1963, the Beach Boys made Billboard's Top 10 list with "Surf City."
Phooey! It was Jan and Dean's song.

HOT OR NOT? Etch-a-Sketch
Hot. This "magic screen" first hit U.S. toy stores in mid-1960; by Christmas millions of American kids had their very own little red-framed tableau.

RAPID RECALL **Q:** How many days did Woodstock last: four, five, or six?
A: Four

ORDER UP! **A.** Lee Harvey Oswald assassinates President John F. Kennedy in Dallas, Texas.
B. Soviet troops invade Czechoslovakia, ending the "Prague Spring."
A. (1963) B. (1968)

HIT PARADE **Q:** What yellow wildflower did The Foundations sing about in their 1969 hit?
A: A buttercup (from "Build me up, Buttercup")

DEAD OR ALIVE? Ritchie Valens
Dead. The budding "La Bamba" singer died alongside Buddy Holly and the Big Bopper in a 1959 plane crash.

BLAST FROM THE PAST

13

FACT OR PHOOEY? In 1960, a first class stamp in the U.S. cost $.04.
Fact.

HOT OR NOT? *Collier's* magazine
Not. This popular publication released its last issue in 1957 after 38 years in print.

RAPID RECALL **Q:** In the 1960s, what school activity did the Supreme Court rule unconstitutional?
A: Prayer

ORDER UP! **A.** Robert Frost recites "The Gift Outright" at John F. Kennedy's inauguration.
B. Nineteen-year-old figure skater Peggy Fleming wins the only U.S. gold at the winter Olympics in Grenoble.
A. (1961) B. (1968)

HIT PARADE **Sing** a line from The Turtles' hit song, "Happy Together."

DEAD OR ALIVE? Jack Benny
Alive. TV's funnyman shtuck around until 1974.

BLAST FROM THE PAST

14

FACT OR PHOOEY?   Earnest Evans changed his name to Fats Domino.
Phooey! He changed it to Chubby Checker.

HOT OR NOT?   *Get Smart*
Hot. This goofy spy show spoof lasted five seasons and won seven Emmys in the mid to late '60s.

RAPID RECALL   **Q:** In 1963, John Glenn became the first American to do what?
A: Orbit the earth

ORDER UP!   **A.** Appointed by President Johnson, Thurgood Marshall is sworn in as the first black U.S. Supreme Court justice.
B. "Itsy Bitsy Teenie Weenie Yellow Polka-Dot Bikini" by Lee Pockriss and Paul Vance makes a splash on the radio waves.
B. (1960) A. (1967)

HIT PARADE   **Q:** Otis Redding sang about wasting time on what in the 1960s?
A: The dock of the bay (from "Sittin' on the Dock of the Bay")

DEAD OR ALIVE?   Joseph McCarthy
Dead. The Senator known for his Communist witch hunts died in 1957.

15

FACT OR PHOOEY? John F. Kennedy, Jr. was born by cesarean section.
Fact.

HOT OR NOT? Astroturf
Hot. This low-maintenance plastic lawn first appeared on the market in 1960, and hit home with suburbanites ready to retire their mowers.

RAPID RECALL **Q:** In the early '60s, President Kennedy started what volunteer group, whose mission is to "promote world peace and friendship"?
A: The Peace Corps

ORDER UP! **A.** Gregory Peck wins an Oscar® for his role as Atticus Finch in *To Kill a Mockingbird*.
B. The price of a Hershey bar doubles ... to 10 cents.
A. (1962) B. (1968)

HIT PARADE **Q:** "They're creepy and they're kooky, mysterious and spooky. They're altogether ooky ..." Who are they?
A: The Addams Family

DEAD OR ALIVE? Bela Lugosi
Dead. "Dracula" died in 1956.

16

FACT OR PHOOEY? In 1960, heavyweight boxer Rocky Marciano won an Olympic gold medal at the Summer Games.
Phooey! Cassius Clay took home the top honor, not Marciano.

HOT OR NOT? "Sit on it!"
Not. Fonzie's phrase didn't catch on till *Happy Days* hit the air in the '70s.

RAPID RECALL **Q:** From what east coast city did the hit TV show *American Bandstand* originate?
A: Philadelphia

ORDER UP! **A.** The FCC bans all cigarette advertising on television and radio.
B. The U.S. Surgeon General report directly links cigarette smoking to cancer for the first time.
B. (1964) A. (1969)

HIT PARADE **Put on your dancing shoes** and do the Watusi. (Don't know it? Make it up!)

DEAD OR ALIVE? Ogden Nash
Alive. Poetry's witty wordsmith rhymed till his time in 1971.

17

FACT OR PHOOEY? Alan Funt was the star of TV's *Rawhide*.
Phooey! He was the host of *Candid Camera*. (Clint Eastwood starred in *Rawhide*.)

HOT OR NOT? *Mystery Date* board game
Hot. *"He's here! My Mystery Date"*—Debuting in 1965, this slumber party staple was an overnight success with young girls across the nation hoping to open the door to a dreamboat.

RAPID RECALL **Q:** Model Twiggy was known for her tiny figure as well as what facial feature?
A: Long eyelashes

ORDER UP! **A.** Half a million people gather in a field near Woodstock, New York for four days of rain, sex, drugs and rock 'n' roll.
B. The Food and Drug administration approves Enovid-10; American women start popping "the Pill" for the first time in the U.S.
B. (1960) A. (1969)

HIT PARADE **Sing** a line from Sonny and Cher's "I Got You Babe."

DEAD OR ALIVE? Tommy Dorsey
Dead. Swing's king buried the band in 1956.

18

FACT OR PHOOEY? Harper Lee wrote the best-selling novel, *Franny and Zooey.*
Phooey! J. D. Salinger wrote about the Glass family in *Franny and Zooey.* (Harper Lee wrote *To Kill A Mockingbird.*)

HOT OR NOT? *Laugh-In*
Hot. Featuring Goldie Hawn and Lily Tomlin, *Laugh-In* had shtick that stuck, enjoying a six-season run.

RAPID RECALL **Q:** What '60s hairstyle does Marge Simpson sport in blue?
A: The beehive

ORDER UP! **A.** The first Jacuzzi heats up in California.
B. *Goldfinger,* starring Sean Connery, debuts at the box office.
B. (1964) A. (1968)

HIT PARADE **Sing** a line from the *George of the Jungle* theme song.

DEAD OR ALIVE? Cecil B. DeMille
Dead. The final cut for Hollywood's head honcho came in 1959.

BLAST FROM THE PAST

19

FACT OR PHOOEY? The Bay of Pigs invasion went exactly as planned.
Phooey! Umm, not exactly.

HOT OR NOT? Poodles
Not. It was the '50s that found images of French poodles on clothing and jewelry, as well as in home décor.

RAPID RECALL Q: What sugar-free soda, the first of its kind, was a hit with dieters when it was introduced in 1963?
A: Tab

ORDER UP! **A.** Faye Dunaway and Warren Beatty glamorize the gun-toting gangsters, Bonnie and Clyde, on the big screen.
B. Children's Television Workshop introduces *Sesame Street* on PBS.
A. (1967) B. (1969)

HIT PARADE Q: What famous music club opened on Hollywood's Sunset Strip in 1963?
A: The Whiskey A-Go-Go

DEAD OR ALIVE? Duane Allman
Alive. Duane died young at age 24, but not until 1971.

BLAST FROM THE PAST

20

FACT OR PHOOEY? Introduced in 1960, Smell-O-Vision! allowed moviegoers to watch and sniff their favorite films.
Fact.

HOT OR NOT? Sit-ins
Hot. Peace. Love. Protest.

RAPID RECALL **Q:** What is the name of Archie's best friend on the cartoon series *The Archie Show*?
A: Jughead Jones

ORDER UP! **A.** Four African American college students demand service at a segregated Woolworth's lunch counter in Greensboro, North Carolina.
B. Ford introduces the sporty Mustang.
A. (1960) B. (1964)

HIT PARADE **Q:** What band scored a hit with their 1963 single "Big Girls Don't Cry," and could also be called Winter, Spring, Summer, and Fall?
A: The Four Seasons

DEAD OR ALIVE? Raymond Chandler
Dead. There's no mystery about it; Chandler's last chapter was written in 1959.

21

FACT OR PHOOEY? The NHL Hockey Hall of Fame opened in Toronto, Canada in 1961.
Fact.

HOT OR NOT? Micro skirts
Hot. Trendy in the late 1960s, the micro raised the mini to racy new heights.

RAPID RECALL **Q:** What are the names of Rocky and Bullwinkle's two Pottsylvanian enemies?
A: Boris and Natasha

ORDER UP! **A.** San Francisco celebrates the Summer of Love.
B. Gary Trudeau's cartoon *Doonesbury* begins syndication.
A. (1967) B. (1969)

HIT PARADE **Q:** What indecipherable one-hit wonder and frat house favorite did The Kingsmen release in 1963?
A: "Louie, Louie"

DEAD OR ALIVE? Mr. Ed
Alive. Oh, Wilbur! TV's famous talking horse got sent to the glue factory in 1979.

BLAST FROM THE PAST

22

FACT OR PHOOEY? Pillsbury purchased Carl's Jr. in 1967.
Phooey! Pillsbury purchased Burger King that year.

HOT OR NOT? Hootenannies
Hot. In the early '60s, folks gathered 'round at these down-home jamborees to sing along with their favorite folksingers.

RAPID RECALL **Q:** How many "Mads" are in the title of the crazy '60s film, *It's a Mad, (etc.) World*?
A: Four

ORDER UP! **A.** Workers complete the St. Louis Gateway Arch.
B. The musical *Hair* dawns on Broadway.
A. (1965) B. (1968)

HIT PARADE **Q:** Fill in the blanks from Buffalo Springfield's hit single: "I think it's time we stop, children, what's that sound? Everybody look, _____ _____ ____."
A: what's goin' down (from "For What It's Worth")

DEAD OR ALIVE? Gladys Presley
Dead. Elvis mourned the loss of his momma in 1958.

BLAST FROM *THE PAST*

23

FACT OR PHOOEY? In 1967, Thurgood Marshall became the first African American appointed to the Supreme Court.
Fact. It was about time!

HOT OR NOT? "What's the word, hummingbird?" (a.k.a. rhyme speak)
Not. This annoying trend took off and trailed off in the late 1940s.

RAPID RECALL Q: What Academy Award® winning actress got her start as Gidget in the popular 1965 TV series?
A: Sally Field

ORDER UP! A. Audrey Hepburn is Holly Golightly on the big screen in *Breakfast at Tiffany's*.
B. Audrey Hepburn stars as Eliza Doolittle in *My Fair Lady*.
A. (1961) B. (1963)

HIT PARADE Q: What animated pop group pushed The Rolling Stones off the top of the charts in 1969?
A: Cartoon characters The Archies scored a hit with "Sugar Sugar," bumping "Honky Tonk Woman" from the top spot.

DEAD OR ALIVE? Ozzie Nelson
Alive. America's favorite father passed away in 1975.

BLAST FROM THE *PAST*

24

FACT OR PHOOEY? Catholics were given the OK to eat unleavened bread on Fridays, except during Lent.
Phooey! They were told that they could eat meat on Fridays.

HOT OR NOT? Nehru jackets
Hot. This collarless fashion statement lasted only a few years in the late 1960s, but was favored by the likes of the Beatles, Joe Namath, and Sammy Davis, Jr.

RAPID RECALL Q: The Disney film, *The Swiss Family Robinson*, was filmed on what island group?
A: The Caribbean

ORDER UP! **A.** Freaked-out fans and Hell's Angels members raise hell at a Rolling Stones concert at the Altamont Speedway in Livermore, California.
B. Bill Cosby's role in *I Spy* makes him the first African American to headline a TV show.
B. (1965) A. (1969)

HIT PARADE Q: According to The Beach Boys, how long can "she" have "Fun, Fun, Fun"?
A: " 'Till her daddy takes the T-Bird away"

DEAD OR ALIVE? Laura Ingalls Wilder (author)
Dead. The lady who brought us the *Little House on the Prairie* series died in 1957.

25

FACT OR PHOOEY? John Denver has been credited with coining the word "groovy."
Fact.

HOT OR NOT? Crewcuts
Not. Also called flattops, these haircuts were hot for guys back in the 1950s.

RAPID RECALL **Q:** *Star Trek*'s Mr. Spock is half human and half what?
A: Vulcan

ORDER UP! **A.** *Peyton Place* premieres on ABC, making television history as the first prime-time soap opera.
B. Muhammad Ali is stripped of his heavyweight title after refusing to join the U.S. Army.
A. (1964) B. (1967)

HIT PARADE **Q:** What was the Beatles' first #1 single in the U.S.?
A: "I Want to Hold Your Hand"

DEAD OR ALIVE? Mary Pickford
Alive. America's old-school sweetheart lived into her 80s, and died in 1979.

BLAST FROM *THE* *PAST*

26

FACT OR PHOOEY?   Flower Power was the hippie equivalent of Black Power.
Fact.

HOT OR NOT?   Turtleneck sweaters
Hot. The good ol' turtleneck was so hip that fashion editors labeled 1967 "The Year of the Turtle."

RAPID RECALL   Q: What famed 1960s football coach asked, "If winning isn't everything, why do they keep score?"
A: Vince Lombardi

ORDER UP!   **A.** *Rolling Stone* magazine hits newsstands for the first time.
B. The Berlin Wall goes up, dividing Germany into East and West.
B. (1961) A. (1967)

HIT PARADE   **Q:** What "Light My Fire" lyric got The Doors in trouble with CBS censors when they sang on *The Ed Sullivan Show*?
A: "Girl, we couldn't get much higher"

DEAD OR ALIVE?   Ezra Pound
Alive. Poetry's epic expatriate survived until 1972.

27

FACT OR PHOOEY? A ring that Jackie Kennedy wore was the inspiration for mood rings.
Phooey!

HOT OR NOT? Chlorophyll
Not. The natural ingredient in plants that makes them green popped up in things like deodorant, toothpaste, insoles, and gum in the 1950s.

RAPID RECALL **Q:** What is the name of Andy Griffith's son on the *Andy Griffith Show*?
A: Opie

ORDER UP! **A.** Simon and Garfunkel release "Mrs. Robinson."
B. Track and field star Wilma Rudolph becomes the first American woman to win three gold medals in the Olympics.
B. (1960) A. (1968)

HIT PARADE **Q:** According to Credence Clearwater Revival, where do Willy and the Poorboys play?
A: Down on the corner, out in the street (from "Down on the Corner")

DEAD OR ALIVE? Ethel Barrymore
Dead. Drew's famous great-aunt pushed up the daisies in 1959.

BLAST FROM THE PAST

28

FACT OR PHOOEY?   Woodstock tickets sold for $36.00 at the gate.
Phooey! They were $24.00.

HOT OR NOT?   *The Power of Positive Thinking*
Not. It was during the 1950s that Norman Vincent Peale's book brought the power to the people.

RAPID RECALL   **Q:** On *Bewitched*, what was Samantha's daughter's name?
A: Tabitha

ORDER UP!   **A.** The Fab Four appear on *The Ed Sullivan Show* and Beatlemania takes the U.S. by storm.
B. *The Godfather* by Mario Puzo hits bookstores.
A. (1964) B. (1969)

HIT PARADE   **Q:** Fill in the blanks in this 1965 Temptations single: "I've got _____ on a cloudy day, when it's cold outside I've got the month of _____."
A: Sunshine; May (from "My Girl")

DEAD OR ALIVE?   Sir Alexander Fleming (scientist)
Dead. The Nobel Prize-winning father of penicillin packed it in 1955.

BLAST FROM THE PAST

29

FACT OR PHOOEY?   In 1963, Tiny Lund won the Daytona 500 without changing his tires.
Fact.

HOT OR NOT?   *The Dick Van Dyke Show*
Hot. Devoted fans followed the lives of young marrieds Rob and Laura Petrie from 1961 to 1966.

RAPID RECALL   **Q:** Which U.S. military service was TV character Gomer Pyle a member of?
A: The Marines

ORDER UP!   **A.** Sonny Liston KOs Floyd Patterson and takes home the world heavyweight boxing title.
B. Prime-time newsmagazine *60 Minutes* premieres on CBS.
A. (1962) B. (1968)

HIT PARADE   **Q:** In 1961, The Shirelles asked if you would still love them . . . when?
A: Tomorrow (from "Will You Still Love Me Tomorrow")

DEAD OR ALIVE?   Hank Williams, Sr.
Dead. Country's legendary crooner died of alcoholism at age 29 in 1953.

BLAST FROM THE PAST

30

FACT OR PHOOEY? Martin Luther King, Jr. and Robert F. Kennedy were both assassinated during the same year.
Fact. The year was 1968.

HOT OR NOT? Tiny Tim
Hot. In his heyday, Tiny Tim had millions of Americans singing along to his 1968 hit, "Tiptoe Through the Tulips," in their best falsettos.

RAPID RECALL Q: How old was Jeannie on the '60s hit, *I Dream of Jeannie:* 26, 100, or 2000 years old?
A: 2000 years old

ORDER UP! A. The miniskirt makes headlines in London.
B. Crosby, Stills, and Nash bag Best New Artist at the Grammys.
A. (1965) B. (1969)

HIT PARADE Q: Fill in the blanks from this 1964 Martha and the Vandellas classic: "Every guy, ____ a girl. Everywhere around ___ _____."
A: Grab; the world (from "Dancing in the Street")

DEAD OR ALIVE? Irene Ryan (*The Beverly Hillbillies'* Granny)
Alive. Granny didn't bite the dust until 1973.

BLAST FROM THE PAST

31

FACT OR PHOOEY? Sally Ride became the first American woman in space during the 1960s.
Phooey! She didn't earn that title until 1983.

HOT OR NOT? Snoods
Not. Female factory workers wore these head coverings in the '50s to keep their hair from getting caught in the machinery.

RAPID RECALL **Q:** What lucky number was painted on the hood of Herbie, the Love Bug?
A: 53

ORDER UP! **A.** The ditto machine suffers a blow when Xerox debuts the first commercial photocopy machine.
B. Congress creates PBS.
A. (1960) B. (1967)

HIT PARADE **Sing** a line from the Righteous Brothers' "You've Lost that Loving Feeling."

DEAD OR ALIVE? Maria Von Trapp
Alive. *The Sound of Music*'s real-life songbird didn't sing her final note until 1987.

BLAST FROM THE PAST

32

FACT OR PHOOEY? In 1964, Malcolm X became the first African American to be named *Time* magazine's "Man of the Year."
Phooey! It was Martin Luther King, Jr.

HOT OR NOT? Pop art
Hot. Though it began in the late 1950s, the likes of Andy Warhol, Jasper Johns, and Roy Lichenstein brought Pop art to the people in the 1960s.

RAPID RECALL **Q:** The classic game Hi-Ho! Cherry-O helped kids of the '60s practice which learning skill?
A: Math/counting

ORDER UP! **A.** Johnny Carson takes over hosting duties of *The Tonight Show.*
B. And the Emmy goes to . . . *The Twilight Zone*'s Rod Serling for outstanding writing achievement in a drama.
B. (1960) A. (1963)

HIT PARADE **Sing** a line of "Are You Lonesome Tonight" in your best Elvis impersonation.

DEAD OR ALIVE? Jack Warner (of Warner Brothers fame)
Alive. Hollywood didn't bury this bigwig until 1978.

BLAST FROM **THE PAST**

33

FACT OR PHOOEY? Audiocassettes originated in Japan.
Phooey! They came from Holland.

HOT OR NOT? *The Avengers*
Hot. The dapper British spy Jonathan Steed and his sexy partner Emma Peel debuted on American TV in 1966.

RAPID RECALL **Q:** Before she had her own show in the '70s, Mary Tyler Moore starred on what Emmy-winning series?
A: *The Dick Van Dyke Show*

ORDER UP! **A.** Marilyn Monroe dies tragically of a drug overdose at age 36.
B. Alfred Hitchcock's *Psycho* scares the bejesus out of moviegoers and rakes in big bucks at the box office.
B. (1960) A. (1962)

HIT PARADE **Q:** Fill in the blanks from Patsy Cline's signature hit "I'm crazy for crying, crazy for trying and I'm crazy for _____ ____."
A: Loving you (from "Crazy")

DEAD OR ALIVE? Errol Flynn
Dead. Hollywood's swashbuckling heartthrob died in 1959.

BLAST FROM THE PAST

34

FACT OR PHOOEY? Zip codes were first used in the U.S. in 1963.
Fact.

HOT OR NOT? "I Like Ike."
Not. Ike was President Eisenhower's nickname and this slogan was used during his 1952 campaign.

RAPID RECALL **Q:** Which bathroom tissue became the best-selling toilet tissue in America due to an ad campaign with Mr. Whipple the grocer?
A: Charmin

ORDER UP! **A.** Arnold Palmer takes top honors at the Masters Tournament for the fourth time.
B. Paul Newman resists the establishment in *Cool Hand Luke*.
A. (1964) B. (1967)

HIT PARADE **Q:** What '80s pop princess brought Tommy James and the Shondells 1967 hit, "I Think We're Alone Now" back to the Top 10?
A: Tiffany

DEAD OR ALIVE? Bruce Lee
Alive. This martial arts master died young, but not until 1973.

BLAST FROM THE PAST

35

FACT OR PHOOEY? Both copy machines and fax machines were introduced during the 1960s.
Fact.

HOT OR NOT? Granny glasses
Hot. John Lennon and The Byrds helped make these hip half-frames a short-lived staple for the style conscious in the mid-'60s.

RAPID RECALL **Q:** What did 16-year-old Bobby Fischer do in 1960?
A: Won the U.S. Chess Championship

ORDER UP! **A.** *Butch Cassidy and the Sundance Kid*'s "Raindrops Keep Fallin' on My Head" walks away with the Oscar® for Best Song.
B. Bob Dylan's "Subterranean Homesick Blues" is released as a single.
B. (1965) A. (1969)

HIT PARADE **Q:** Fill in the blanks in the 1969 Jeanie C. Reilly song about small town hypocrites: "... the day my mama socked it to the _____ _____ P.T.A."
A: Harper Valley (from "Harper Valley P.T.A.")

DEAD OR ALIVE? Lou Costello (of Abbott and Costello)
Dead. This "Who's on First?" funnyman died in 1959.

BLAST FROM THE PAST

36

FACT OR PHOOEY? Hairstylist Paul McGregor invented the shag carpet in 1965.
Phooey! McGregor invented the shag haircut, which featured hair cropped close to the head and longer wispy pieces at the sides and nape of the neck.

HOT OR NOT? Transcendental meditation
Not. Though introduced in the 1960s, Transcendental meditation didn't really reach its zenith till the mid-70s.

RAPID RECALL **Q:** Washington state's Space Needle and Monorail were built as part of what event in 1962?
A: The World's Fair

ORDER UP! **A.** The Nobel Peace Prize goes to Martin Luther King, Jr.
B. JFK advises "prudent families" to build bomb shelters in their backyards.
B. (1961) A. (1964)

HIT PARADE **Sing** a line (other than the na-na-na's) from The Beatles' song that set a new record for length of a radio single in 1968.
A: "Hey Jude." The song clocked in at a then unheard-of seven minutes and seven seconds.

DEAD OR ALIVE? Samuel Goldwyn
Alive. Born Samuel Goldfish, this Hollywood hotshot hung on until 1974.

BLAST FROM THE PAST

37

FACT OR PHOOEY?   *The Hustler* is a movie about male gigolos.
Phooey! It's about pool players.

HOT OR NOT?   *The Many Loves of Dobie Gillis*
Hot. This groundbreaking '60s teen sitcom helped launch the careers of Warren Beatty, Bob Denver, and Tuesday Weld.

RAPID RECALL   **Q:** What was Jed Clampett on *The Beverly Hillbillies* doing when he discovered bubblin' crude, or oil?
A: Shootin' (at some food)

ORDER UP!   **A.** John Steinbeck wins the Pulitzer prize for literature.
B. Kurt Vonnegut publishes *Slaughterhouse Five*.
A. (1962) B. (1969)

HIT PARADE   **Q:** Fill in the blanks from this Peter, Paul, and Mary song that flew to the top of the charts: "So kiss me and smile for me, tell me that ___ ___ ___ ___."
A: You'll wait for me (from "Leaving on a Jet Plane")

DEAD OR ALIVE?   Mel Ott
Dead. The New York Giants' baseball great struck out in 1959.

BLAST FROM THE PAST

38

FACT OR PHOOEY? *Lawrence of Arabia* cost $33 million to make and was panned by critics.
Phooey! The film only cost $13 million and won seven Oscars®.

HOT OR NOT? *Mister Magoo*
Hot. The myopic cartoon character had his own TV show during 1964 and 1965.

RAPID RECALL Q: Which American icon made the pillbox hat popular in the '60s?
A: Jacqueline Kennedy

ORDER UP! **A.** The first U.S. combat troops arrive in Vietnam.
B. Dr. Christiaan N. Barnard and a team of South African surgeons perform the world's first successful human heart transplant.
A. (1965) B. (1967)

HIT PARADE Q: The ballad of what military organization kept Sergeant Barry Sadler firmly at the top of the charts for five weeks in 1966?
A: "The Ballad of the Green Berets"

DEAD OR ALIVE? Frank Lloyd Wright
Dead. America's premier architect, known for his Prairie Style, died in 1959.

BLAST FROM THE PAST

39

FACT OR PHOOEY? In *Birdman of Alcatraz*, Burt Lancaster plays an escaped convict who gets pecked to death by a flock of canaries.
Phooey! Lancaster's character never escapes, and his beloved birds wouldn't peck a fly.

HOT OR NOT? Flagpole perching
Not. Its popularity peaked in 1946 when a couple said their vows on top of a flagpole.

RAPID RECALL **Q:** Published in 1987, Pamela Des Barres' tell-all book *I'm With the Band* talks about her life as a 1960s what?
A: Rock groupie

ORDER UP! **A.** *West Side Story* wins Best Picture at the Oscars®.
B. Protests erupt and draft cards are burned on national "Turn in Your Draft Card Day."
A. (1961) B. (1968)

HIT PARADE **Sing** a line from Neil Sedaka's 1962 hit about the difficulties of ending a relationship.
A: "Breaking Up is Hard to Do"

DEAD OR ALIVE? Juan Peron
Alive. The former president of Argentina and husband of Evita died in 1974.

BLAST FROM THE PAST

40

FACT OR PHOOEY? Spencer Tracy won an Oscar® for his last movie *Guess Who's Coming to Dinner?*
Phooey! Spencer did not get the nod from the Academy, but his co-star Katherine Hepburn did.

HOT OR NOT? Marathon bed pushing
Hot. In the early 1960s, this brief craze had bed-headed pranksters wheeling souped-up mattresses across the county.

RAPID RECALL Q: What detective TV series featured television's first female police officer?
A: *The Mod Squad*

ORDER UP! **A.** Betty Friedan founds the National Organization for Women.
B. The Academy awards *Mary Poppins'* "Chim Chim Cher-ee" the Oscar® for Best Song.
B. (1963) A. (1966)

HIT PARADE Q: Poor Dion. In 1961, he complained about a girl who took his love and then ran around with other boys. Who was she?
A: Runaround Sue

DEAD OR ALIVE? Margaret Mead
Alive. Anthropology's over-achiever didn't go to her grave until 1978.

BLAST FROM THE PAST

41

FACT OR PHOOEY? TV's *Gomer Pyle, USMC* was a spin-off of *The Andy Griffith Show.*
Fact.

HOT OR NOT? Weejuns
Hot. These penny loafer shoes made by Bass were filled with bare feet in the 1960s.

RAPID RECALL **Q:** What is the title of the first James Bond movie, released in 1962?
A: *Dr. No*

ORDER UP! **A.** Ray Kroc purchases the McDonald brothers' restaurant chain, opening 200 burger joints in Southern California.
B. "And now for something completely different . . ." *Monty Python's Flying Circus* debuts on BBC.
A. (1961) B. (1969)

HIT PARADE **Q:** In 1962, The Contours asked, "Do you love me, now that I can dance?" What two dances could they do?
A: The Mashed Potato and the Twist (from "Do You Love Me?")

DEAD OR ALIVE? Duke Ellington
Alive. This jazz great tickled the keys until 1974.

BLAST FROM THE PAST

42

FACT OR PHOOEY? In 1961, New York teams won both the Super Bowl and the World Series.
Phooey! The Yankees clinched the World Series against Cincinnati, but the Giants got clobbered by the Green Bay Packers.

HOT OR NOT? Bean bag chairs
Not. Comfortable and colorful, this was where '70s discoers parked themselves after a long night on the dance floor.

RAPID RECALL Q: Pop artist Robert Indiana created a sculpture forming what word?
A: Love

ORDER UP! A. The Kennedy half-dollar is the newest currency.
B. Bille Jean King scores her third Wimbledon title.
A. (1964) B. (1968)

HIT PARADE Q: From what camp was Allan Sherman writing, "Hello Muddah, Hello Faddah" when he sang his famous letter home in 1963?
A: Camp Grenada

DEAD OR ALIVE? Connie Mack
Dead. This baseball Hall of Famer hung up his bat in 1956.

BLAST FROM
THE PAST

43

FACT OR PHOOEY? In the '60s, "far out" was another way of saying things were cool; it was also slang for "thanks."
Fact.

HOT OR NOT? Twister
Hot. Twister became a bona fide fad on May 3, 1966 after Johnny Carson played a game with scantily clad Eva Gabor on *The Tonight Show*.

RAPID RECALL **Q:** What profession does Truly Scrumptious' father practice in the movie *Chitty Chitty Bang Bang*?
A: Candymaker

ORDER UP! **A.** Federal deputy marshals escort four African American girls into the first desegregated schools in Louisiana.
B. 25-year-old Cassius Clay defeats Sonny Liston, winning the World Heavyweight title.
A. (1960) B. (1964)

HIT PARADE **Q:** According to Manfred Man, "she looked good, she looked fine" while walking down the street. **Sing** the line she sang.
A: "Do wah diddy diddy dum diddy do"

DEAD OR ALIVE? Jackson Pollock
Dead. Pollock packed up his paintbrush in 1956.

BLAST FROM THE PAST

44

FACT OR PHOOEY? On an Etch-a-Sketch, the right knob controls the horizontal movement and the left knob controls the vertical movement.
Phooey! Left is horizontal and right is vertical.

HOT OR NOT? *The Burns and Allen Show*
Not. George and Gracie's TV show made audiences laugh from 1950 to 1958.

RAPID RECALL **Q:** What type of beads did teens in the '60s love to sport around their necks as a symbol of friendship?
A: Love beads

ORDER UP! **A.** The Green Bay Packers clobber the Kansas City Chiefs in Super Bowl I, 35-10.
B. Berry Gordy borrows $800 and launches Motown Records.
B. (1960) A. (1967)

HIT PARADE **Sing** (or hum) the guitar riff of the Rolling Stone's "Can't Get No Satisfaction."

DEAD OR ALIVE? Henri Matisse
Dead. Matisse painted his last stroke in 1954.

BLAST FROM **THE PAST**

45

FACT OR PHOOEY? In 1965, U.S. scientists made headlines when they took the first close-up pictures of Uranus.
Phooey! The close-ups were of Mars.

HOT OR NOT? The Jitterbug
Not. Cab Calloway recorded the song and hepcats danced to it throughout the late 1930s and early 1940s.

RAPID RECALL Q: What perennial pinball favorite, released by Gottlieb in 1963, was designed to capitalize on the popularity of Playboy Clubs?
A: Slick Chick

ORDER UP! A. Milwaukee-raised Golda Meir becomes the new Prime Minister of Israel.
B. "Papa" Hemingway commits suicide with a shotgun.
B. (1961) A. (1969)

HIT PARADE Q: Fill in the blanks of this Leiber and Stoller classic that hit the charts in 1965: "She's got a little pad down on Thirty-Fourth and _____, selling little bottles of love potion _____ _____."
A: Vine; Number Nine (from "Love Potion Number Nine")

DEAD OR ALIVE? Alexander Calder (American sculptor)
Alive. Calder didn't hang it up until 1976.

46

FACT OR PHOOEY?   Milton Bradley introduced the game Operation® in 1965.
Fact.

HOT OR NOT?   Smiley-face buttons
Hot. They made their way onto everything from jewelry to furniture before fading away in the mid 1970s.

RAPID RECALL   **Q:** What comedic actor played Clem Kadiddlehopper, Freddie the Freeloader, and the Mean Widdle Kid?
A: Red Skelton

ORDER UP!   **A.** Barbra Streisand stars in *Funny Girl* on Broadway.
B. John Lennon and Yoko Ono tie the knot, head to Amsterdam, and stage a weeklong "lie-in" for peace.
A. (1964) B. (1968)

HIT PARADE   **Q:** What famous Dennis Hopper flick featured Steppenwolf's rock anthem, "Born to be Wild"?
A: *Easy Rider*

DEAD OR ALIVE?   George Reeves (TV's original *Superman*)
Dead. This superhero died in 1959.

BLAST FROM THE PAST

47

FACT OR PHOOEY? *Apollo II* landed on the moon in July 1969.
Fact.

HOT OR NOT? Courreges fashions
Hot. "Space fashions" were the specialty of this famous French fashion house.

RAPID RECALL **Q:** What 1966 book written by Jacqueline Susann featured three young women clawing their way to the top, and hitting bottom, in New York City?
A: *Valley of the Dolls*

ORDER UP! **A.** Pampers introduces the first disposable diaper.
B. 40 "Dead Sea" scrolls are unearthed in Palestine.
B. (1961) A. (1966)

HIT PARADE **Sing** a line from Aretha Franklin's 1967 signature song with a built-in spelling lesson.
A: "Respect"

DEAD OR ALIVE? Louella Parsons (Hollywood gossip columnist)
Alive. Rumor has it that this well-known chitchatter died in 1972.

BLAST FROM THE PAST

48

FACT OR PHOOEY? The polio vaccine became available for use in 1969.
Phooey! The measles vaccine hit the market in '69; the polio vaccine had already been around since the mid-50s.

HOT OR NOT? Little white Go-Go boots
Hot. Most associated with Nancy Sinatra and her anthem, "These Boots Are Made For Walking," they were all the rage in the mid-1960s.

RAPID RECALL **Q:** What nickname did American soldiers give to Vietcong guerillas fighting in South Vietnam during the Viet Nam war?
A: Charlie

ORDER UP! **A.** White South African officials sentence Nelson Mandela to prison.
B. Amana introduces U.S. consumers to the first microwave oven; the Radar Range sells for $495.
A. (1964) B. (1967)

HIT PARADE **Q:** During 1967's Summer of Love, what did singer Scott McKenzie tell San Francisco-bound people to wear in their hair?
A: Flowers (from "San Francisco (Be Sure to Wear Flowers in Your Hair)")

DEAD OR ALIVE? Charlie Parker
Dead. The "Bird" blew his last note in 1955.

BLAST FROM THE PAST

49

FACT OR PHOOEY?   Patty Duke played identical cousins Kathy and Patty on TV's *The Patty Duke Show.*
Fact.

HOT OR NOT?   "Whatever turns you on."
Hot. This 1960s catch phrase implied freedom to do whatever.

RAPID RECALL   **Q:** In 1966, what famed lawyer got Sam Sheppard's guilty verdict reversed ten years after the original judgment?
A: F. Lee Bailey

ORDER UP!   **A.** J. Edgar Hoover launches an FBI counterintelligence program against the Black Panther Party.
B. Scientist Rachel Carson blows the lid off of insecticides with the publication of *Silent Spring.*
B. (1962) A. (1968)

HIT PARADE   **Q:** The Monkees had two hit singles in 1967 with the word "believer" in the titles. What were they?
A: "Daydream Believer" and "I'm a Believer"

DEAD OR ALIVE?   Bing Crosby
Alive. The crooner with the velvet voice didn't croak until 1977.

BLAST FROM THE PAST

50

FACT OR PHOOEY? *The Donna Reed Show*'s Shelley Fabares had a 1962 hit with "Johnny Angel."
Fact.

HOT OR NOT? Beaded curtains
Not. These groovy curtains decorated doorways instead of windows in the 1970s.

RAPID RECALL Q: What actor portrayed Doctor Doolittle in the 1968 musical movie release?
A: Rex Harrison

ORDER UP! A. Nikita Khrushchev gets peevish and pounds his shoe on a desk at a United Nations meeting.
B. The Beatles play their last live concert in San Francisco's Candlestick Park.
A. (1960) B. (1966)

HIT PARADE Q: In what 1964 hit did the Beatles claim they'd been working like dogs and should be sleeping like logs?
A: "A Hard Day's Night"

DEAD OR ALIVE? Charlie Chaplin
Alive. This Hollywood legend lived a long life and passed away in 1977.

BLAST FROM THE PAST

51

FACT OR PHOOEY? The 1968 Summer Olympics were held in Montreal, Canada.
Phooey! In '68, the Summer Games were held in Mexico City, Mexico; the Winter Games were in Grenoble, France.

HOT OR NOT? Masters and Johnson
Hot. Their revolutionary 1966 publication, *Human Sexual Response,* changed the way that Americans thought about sex.

RAPID RECALL **Q:** What did the Flintstones call their "dog"?
A: Dino (who is actually a dinosaur)

ORDER UP! **A.** A riot in New York's Stonewall Inn launches the Gay and Lesbian Rights movement.
B. Bolivian troops capture and kill Latin American revolutionary icon Che Guevara.
B. (1967) A (1969)

HIT PARADE **Q:** What "brand-new dance" was Little Eva teaching people how to do in 1962?
A: The Loco-Motion

DEAD OR ALIVE? Eliot Ness (crime fighter)
Dead. Al Capone's captor gave up the ghost in 1957.

BLAST FROM THE PAST

52

FACT OR PHOOEY? Coffee Mate came to the U.S. in 1961, though it had been sold in Italy as Café Amici since 1959.
Phooey! The first non-dairy creamer was initially sold in the U.S.

HOT OR NOT? Kaftans
Hot. Hippies donned these Moroccan-inspired dresses.

RAPID RECALL **Q:** Who are Salvatore and Cherilyn better known as?
A: Sony and Cher

ORDER UP! **A.** Civil rights leader Stokely Carmichael coins the phrase "Black Power."
B. American poet Sylvia Plath commits suicide in London.
B. (1963) A. (1967)

HIT PARADE **Sing** a line from Nancy Sinatra's footwear-centered hit.
A: "These Boots Are Made for Walking"

DEAD OR ALIVE? Erich von Stroheim
Dead. This director and *Sunset Boulevard* star died in 1957 at the age of 71.

BLAST FROM THE PAST

53

FACT OR PHOOEY? The World Health Organization's mission to eradicate the smallpox virus began in 1966.
Fact.

HOT OR NOT? Don Kirshner's Rock Concert
Not. Kirshner gave big name rock bands a late-night timeslot, but not until 1973.

RAPID RECALL **Q:** What is the title of Dr. Martin Luther King's famous Washington, D.C. speech?
A: *I Have a Dream*

ORDER UP! **A.** *Gunsmoke* is number one on TV.
B. Police attack anti-war protestors outside the Democratic National Convention in Chicago, Illinois.
A. (1960) B. (1968)

HIT PARADE **Q:** Who exchanged glances in Frank Sinatra's 1966 hit?
A: Strangers in the night

DEAD OR ALIVE? Pablo Picasso
Alive. The artist credited with inventing Cubism didn't die until 1973.

BLAST FROM THE PAST

54

FACT OR PHOOEY? George Jetson works at Cogswell's Cogs.
Phooey! Jetson works for Spacely's Sprockets; Cogswell's Cogs is the competition.

HOT OR NOT? Op Art
Hot. Optical Art featured trippy colors and pictures that appeared to move.

RAPID RECALL **Q:** What rotund rocker inspired '60s teens to "do the Twist"?
A: Chubby Checker

ORDER UP! **A.** President Johnson announces he won't run for re-election.
B. Grateful Dead front man Jerry Garcia celebrates his twentieth birthday.
B. (1962) A. (1968)

HIT PARADE **Put on your dancing shoes** and do the Swim. (Don't know it? Make it up!)

DEAD OR ALIVE? Richard E. Byrd (Antarctic explorer)
Dead. Byrd embarked on his final expedition in 1957.

55

FACT OR PHOOEY? In 1969, young Americans did a new dance called the "Apollo" to commemorate the first landing on the moon.
Fact.

HOT OR NOT? The New York Giants baseball team
Not. The Giants said goodbye to the Big Apple and hello to San Francisco back in 1958.

RAPID RECALL **Q:** Who was once just "a little green slab of clay," and originally appeared on *Howdy Doody* before getting his own show in 1966?
A: Gumby

ORDER UP! **A.** President Eisenhower wraps up his second (and final) term in the White House.
B. Black nationalist leader Malcolm X is assassinated at a Harlem rally.
A. (1961) B. (1964)

HIT PARADE **Sing** a line from the *Green Acres* theme song.

DEAD OR ALIVE? Arturo Toscanini
Dead. Italy's renowned conductor bowed out in 1957.

BLAST FROM **THE PAST**

56

FACT OR PHOOEY? Amnesty International was started in 1961.
Fact.

HOT OR NOT? Zoot Suits
Not. These overstated suits were the height of Hepcat fashion back in the early 1940s.

RAPID RECALL **Q:** What is Speed Racer's girlfriend's name?
A: Trixie

ORDER UP! **A.** The Cuban missile crisis hits home and pushes the U.S. to the brink of a nuclear war with the Soviet Union.
B. *Hawaii Five-O* makes a splash on CBS.
A. (1962) B. (1968)

HIT PARADE **Q:** According to Bob Dylan, where was the answer blowin'?
A: In the wind (from "Blowin' in the Wind")

DEAD OR ALIVE? Oliver Hardy
Dead. Laurel's famous sidekick kept 'em laughing until 1957.

FACT OR PHOOEY? In *Barefoot in the Park*, Robert Redford wears a garbage can like a hat.
Fact. He does it while he's dancing barefoot.

HOT OR NOT? Ducktails
Hot. Many men of the early '60s, including Elvis, sported this greased-back hairstyle that resembled the tail end of a duck.

RAPID RECALL **Q:** What household appliance did girls use to straighten their hair in the late '60s?
A: The iron

ORDER UP! **A.** *Planet of the Apes* swings into theaters.
B. Frank Sinatra and Mia Farrow tie the knot in a Las Vegas ceremony.
B. (1966) A. (1968)

HIT PARADE **Q:** Who hit number one in 1964 with the song "Pretty Woman"?
A: Roy Orbison

DEAD OR ALIVE? Dame Agatha Christie (author)
Alive. England's illustrious murder mystery writer didn't die until 1976.

1970s

1

FACT OR PHOOEY? Jane Seymour once played a Bond girl named Solitaire.
Fact. It was in the first Roger Moore Bond movie, *Live and Let Die.*

HOT OR NOT? Talking to plants
Hot. In the early '70s, people not only talked to their plants, they nurtured them with George Milstein's hit record, *Music to Grow Plants By.*

RAPID RECALL **Q:** List the names of the three Brady Bunch boys from youngest to oldest.
A: Bobby, Peter, Greg

ORDER UP! **A.** An explosion aboard Apollo 13 forces the crew to make an emergency splashdown in the Pacific Ocean.
B. The Shah of Iran escapes for a "vacation" after a year of turmoil; the Ayatollah Khomeini takes command.
A. (1970) B. (1979)

HIT PARADE **Q:** In 1970, Ernie made it into the Top 20 with what ode to his favorite toy?
A: "Rubber Duckie"

DEAD OR ALIVE? Grace Kelly
Alive. Hitchcock's muse and Monaco's princess met her tragic end in 1982.

BLAST FROM THE PAST

2

FACT OR PHOOEY? *Up In Smoke* was one of the last great Westerns.
Phooey! It was a Cheech and Chong flick.

HOT OR NOT? Leisure suits
Hot. Yes, polyester really was hot at one time.

RAPID RECALL **Q:** What Italian import became popular in the U.S. during the 1970s, partially due to the national fuel crisis during this time?
A: The moped

ORDER UP! **A.** Former Georgia governor Jimmy Carter defeats Gerald Ford in the race for the White House.
B. The U.S. Supreme Court unanimously upholds school busing for desegregation.
B. (1971) A. (1976)

HIT PARADE **Q:** According to Janis Joplin's "Me and Bobby McGee": "Freedom's just another word for _____ left to ____."
A: Nothing; lose

DEAD OR ALIVE? Steve McQueen
Alive. *The Great Escape* star didn't make his final exit until 1980.

BLAST FROM
THE PAST

3

FACT OR PHOOEY? Gilda Radner appeared in *Blazing Saddles.*
Fact. It's true, though her name doesn't appear in the credits.

HOT OR NOT? Rubber clothing
Not. These clothes were made by designers like Jean-Paul Gaultier in the 1980s and 1990s.

RAPID RECALL Ω: What television show was the first to feature an interracial couple?
A: *The Jeffersons*

ORDER UP! **A.** President Carter and Soviet head Leonid Brezhnev sign the second Strategic Arms Limitation Treaty (SALT II) agreement.
B. Kids play their very first arcade video game, "Pong," introduced by Atari.
B. (1972) A. (1979)

HIT PARADE **Sing** a line from The Five Stairsteps' hit "Ooh Child."

DEAD OR ALIVE? Boris Karloff
Dead. Famous for his *Frankenstein,* this king of horror died in 1969.

BLAST FROM THE PAST

4

FACT OR PHOOEY? Guitarist Ron Wood quit the Rolling Stones in 1974 and was replaced by Mick Taylor.
Phooey! Scratch that, reverse it—Wood replaced Taylor.

HOT OR NOT? *The Joy of Sex*
Hot. Dr. Alex Comfort wrote this very popular "gourmet guide to lovemaking."

RAPID RECALL **Q:** Which Apollo brought back rock and soil samples from the moon in the '70s: Apollo 7, 13, or 17?
A: Apollo 17

ORDER UP! **A.** Muhammad Ali takes back the world heavyweight title in the "Rumble in the Jungle" against George Foreman.
B. *Saturday Night Fever* sparks the disco inferno.
A. (1974) B. (1977)

HIT PARADE **Q:** In Three Dog Night's "Joy to the World," what was Jeremiah?
A: A bullfrog

DEAD OR ALIVE? Meyer Lansky (mobster)
Alive. The mythical Meyer didn't pack it in till 1983.

BLAST FROM THE PAST

5

FACT OR PHOOEY? *Adam 12* was a TV show about firefighters.
Phooey! It was about police officers.

HOT OR NOT? *The Green Hornet*
Not. This cult favorite aired in the mid-60s, and featured Bruce Lee as the martial arts bodyguard named Kato.

RAPID RECALL **Q:** What union is Ceasar Chavez credited with founding?
A: Farm Workers Union

ORDER UP! **A.** 14-year-old Romanian gymnast Nadia Comaneci scores seven perfect 10s and pockets three gold medals.
B. Prime-time soap and pop-culture phenomenon *Dallas* kicks off on CBS.
A. (1976) B. (1978)

HIT PARADE **Q:** What three types of social outcasts are the title subjects of Cher's 1971 number one hit?
A: Gypsies, tramps, and thieves

DEAD OR ALIVE? Clara Bow
Dead. Hollywood's original "It Girl" turned up her toes in 1965.

BLAST FROM THE PAST

6

FACT OR PHOOEY? The Chrysler Corporation was given $1.5 billion in Federal aid in 1979.
Fact.

HOT OR NOT? Sea Monkeys
Hot. These scientific marvels were one of the coolest things a kid could own in the 1970s.

RAPID RECALL Q: In what neighborhood of Niagara Falls, New York were residents evacuated because of dangerous toxins buried in their soil?
A: Love Canal

ORDER UP! **A.** Louise Brown, the world's first test-tube baby, is born in London.
B. A federal jury acquits the "Chicago Seven" of conspiracy to riot during the 1968 Democratic National Convention.
B. (1970) A. (1978)

HIT PARADE Q: What singer/songwriter tasted Top 40 success with "American Pie" in 1971?
A: Don McLean

DEAD OR ALIVE? Mae West
Alive. West kept 'em coming up to see her until her death in 1980.

BLAST FROM **THE** PAST

7

FACT OR PHOOEY? In *The Godfather,* James Caan plays the Corleone son, Fredo. Phooey! Caan plays Sonny (Santino).

HOT OR NOT? *Miami Vice*
Not. Don Johnson and Philip Michael Thomas sported their casual pastel clothing during the 1980s.

RAPID RECALL **Q:** What was the name of reggae singer Bob Marley's band?
A: The Wailers

ORDER UP! **A.** The U.S. celebrates its bicentennial and releases a special commemorative quarter.
B. Egyptian President Anwar al-Sadat and Israeli Prime Minister Menachem Begin sign a "Framework for Peace" after a 13-day powwow with President Carter.
A. (1976) B. (1978)

HIT PARADE **Sing** a line from the Credence Clearwater Revival song that Ike and Tina Turner took to number four on the charts in 1971.
(A: "Proud Mary")

DEAD OR ALIVE? Nat King Cole
Dead. This unforgettable singer died in 1965.

BLAST FROM THE PAST

8

FACT OR PHOOEY? The movie *American Graffiti* and TV's *Happy Days* both feature Henry Winkler.
Phooey! They both feature Ron Howard.

HOT OR NOT? Green and orange home décor
Hot. Many homes sported the "Halloween meets St. Patrick's Day" look in everything from orange sofas to wall-to-wall green shag.

RAPID RECALL Q: What singer claims her band's name came from the repeated catcalls she got from New York City truck drivers?
A: Blondie

ORDER UP! A. President Ford survives two assassination attempts, both made by women.
B. Pete Rose sets a National League consecutive game hitting streak record of 44.
A. (1975) B. (1978)

HIT PARADE Q: Name this tune and the band who wrote it: "There's a lady who's sure/ All that glitters is gold/ And she's buying the..."
A: "Stairway to Heaven" (by Led Zeppelin)

DEAD OR ALIVE? Alfred Hitchcock
Alive. Hitchcock kept us in suspense till 1980.

BLAST FROM THE PAST

9

FACT OR PHOOEY? In 1971, a priest was charged with conspiracy to kidnap Henry Kissinger.
Fact.

HOT OR NOT? Mohair suits
Hot. Elton John favored these scratchy suits, and even paid tribute to them in "Benny and the Jets."

RAPID RECALL **Q:** What color is Farrah Fawcett's bathing suit in her famous pin-up poster?
A: Red

ORDER UP! **A.** A nuclear meltdown at Pennsylvania's Three Mile Island threatens local communities.
B. Maya Angelou publishes *I Know Why the Caged Bird Sings*.
B. (1970) A. (1979)

HIT PARADE **Q:** Fill in the blanks in this 1970 Top 10 hit "Baby, I'll be there to hold your hand, Baby, I'll be there to share the____."
A: Land (by The Guess Who, from "Share the Land")

DEAD OR ALIVE? Joe Louis (professional boxer)
Alive. The man who helped KO racial barriers in the sports world stayed around the ring until 1981.

BLAST FROM THE PAST

10

FACT OR PHOOEY? In *Shampoo*, Warren Beatty plays a Beverly Hills hairdresser.
Fact.

HOT OR NOT? The *Batman* TV show
Not. Holy Nielsen Ratings! This campy show aired from 1966 – 1968 and featured many celebrity guest stars.

RAPID RECALL **Q:** If you had the Jordache look, what animal was stitched onto the logo of your jeans?
A: A pony (or horse)

ORDER UP! **A.** Ryan O'Neal and Ali McGraw star in *Love Story*.
B. *The Love Boat* sets sail on ABC with Gavin MacLeod as the captain.
A. (1970) B. (1977)

HIT PARADE **Sing** a line from the John Lennon song that asked music listeners to play pretend in 1971.
A: "Imagine"

DEAD OR ALIVE? Clark Gable
Dead. Hollywood's heartthrob died young at the age of 59 in 1960.

11

FACT OR PHOOEY? TV detective Columbo is known for always sucking on a lollipop.
Phooey! Kojak has the lollipop fetish.

HOT OR NOT? Platform shoes
Hot. These treacherous shoes were literally the height of '70s fashion.

RAPID RECALL **Q:** Where does Snoopy find his previous owner in *Snoopy, Come Home*?
A: A hospital

ORDER UP! **A.** The U.S. Supreme Court kills the death penalty, citing it as "cruel and unusual" punishment.
B. Convicted murderer Gary Gilmore faces the firing squad in the first U.S. execution in 10 years.
A. (1972) B. (1977)

HIT PARADE **Q:** What two musical ailments was Johnny Rivers suffering from in 1972?
A: Rocking Pneumonia and the Boogie Woogie Flu

DEAD OR ALIVE? Ira Gershwin
Alive. With his brother George, Gershwin composed musicals like *Porgy and Bess* before dying in 1983.

12

FACT OR PHOOEY? Daisy®, introduced in 1975, was the first disposable razor for women.
Fact. It was made by Gillette.

HOT OR NOT? Bouffant hairdo
Not. This high-maintenance hairstyle died out in the late '60s.

RAPID RECALL Q: Which child is the first to be eliminated in the movie *Willie Wonka and the Chocolate Factory*?
A: Augustus Gloop

ORDER UP! A. *Life* magazine calls it quits after 36 years in print.
B. Over 900 followers of the Reverend Jim Jones commit mass suicide in Jonestown, Guyana.
A. (1972) B. (1978)

HIT PARADE Q: In 1972, the members of America went "through the desert on a _____ with no _____."
A: Horse; name (from "A Horse With No Name")

DEAD OR ALIVE? Tennessee Williams
Alive. The playwright of *A Streetcar Named Desire* died in 1983.

13

FACT OR PHOOEY? Leslie Ann Warren plays Janet in *The Rocky Horror Picture Show.*
Phooey! Susan Sarandon played Janet.

HOT OR NOT? *The Man from U.N.C.L.E.*
Not. This mid-60s spy show went off the air in 1968.

RAPID RECALL Ω: What popular 1970s fragrance slogan suggested women could "bring home the bacon, fry it up in a pan, and never let you forget you're a man"?
A: Enjoli

ORDER UP! **A.** George C. Scott snubs the Academy and turns down his Best Actor Oscar® for *Patton.*
B. 33-year-old Robert Opal livens up the Oscars® by streaking across the stage naked on national TV.
A. (1970) B. (1974)

HIT PARADE Ω: What fictional familial rockers had a hit on the charts before the world saw the first episode of their television show?
A: The Partridge Family

DEAD OR ALIVE? Maxfield Parrish (artist)
Dead. Parrish perished in 1966, but his work lives on in museums around the world.

BLAST FROM THE PAST

14

FACT OR PHOOEY? John Travolta had a regular role on TV's *Little House on the Prairie*.
Phooey! Travolta was a regular on *Welcome Back, Kotter*.

HOT OR NOT? *Détente*
Hot. Politians tossed around this term that described the easing of tensions between nations, especially between the post–Cold War Soviet Union and the United States.

RAPID RECALL **Q:** In *Pete's Dragon*, what magical power does Elliot possess?
A: He can make himself invisible.

ORDER UP! **A.** 63 Americans are taken hostage at the U.S. embassy in Tehran.
B. Congress approves the Equal Rights Amendment, but it fails to be ratified by the states.
B. (1972) A. (1979)

HIT PARADE **Q:** Carole King, who spent the Sixties writing hits for other people, broke out on her own with what 1971 album?
A: *Tapestry*

DEAD OR ALIVE? Gloria Swanson (actress)
Alive. Swanson took her swan dive in 1983.

BLAST FROM THE PAST

15

FACT OR PHOOEY? Laverne and Shirley worked at the Shotz Brewery with Lenny and Squiggy.
Fact.

HOT OR NOT? Lava lamps
Hot. And groovy, too.

RAPID RECALL Q: Which television network did kids rush home to watch for its *Afterschool Special* series, which mixed education with entertainment?
A: ABC

ORDER UP! **A.** Viking I sends video postcards from Mars.
B. Voyager sends home snapshots of Jupiter.
A. (1976) B. (1979)

HIT PARADE Q: Where were Gladys Knight and the Pips taking a midnight train to in 1973?
A: Georgia (from "Midnight Train to Georgia")

DEAD OR ALIVE? Walt Disney
Dead. The beloved "Imagineer" died before his time in 1966.

BLAST FROM THE PAST

16

FACT OR PHOOEY? President Nixon granted unconditional amnesty to Vietnam War draft dodgers.
Phooey! President Carter did it.

HOT OR NOT? Barbers
Not. They became "hair stylists" in the early 1970s.

RAPID RECALL **Q:** What kids' TV show regularly aired *The Adventures of Spidey,* which featured short clips of the superhero in action?
A: *The Electric Company*

ORDER UP! **A.** *Star Wars* storms into theaters.
B. Francis Ford Coppola scores a hit with *The Godfather.*
B. (1972) A. (1977)

HIT PARADE **Sing** a line from The Carpenters' 1973 single "Top of the World."

DEAD OR ALIVE? Jack Dempsey (professional boxer)
Alive. One of the world's all-time greatest heavyweight boxers died in 1983.

BLAST FROM *THE PAST*

17

FACT OR PHOOEY? Two elected Popes died in 1978.
Fact.

HOT OR NOT? *Kukla, Fran, and Ollie*
Not. This hugely popular kids' show featuring puppets ended in 1957.

RAPID RECALL **Q:** Who was the youngest member of The Osmonds as seen on
The Osmond Show in the '70s?
A: Jimmy Osmond

ORDER UP! **A.** Elvis Presley passes away at Graceland, his Memphis mansion.
B. Guitar god Jimi Hendrix dies at age 27.
B. (1970) A. (1977)

HIT PARADE **Q:** Name the song that first put Aerosmith on the musical map.
A: "Dream On"

DEAD OR ALIVE? Count Basie (musician)
Alive. The great swing conductor and jazz pianist died in 1984.

BLAST FROM THE PAST

18

FACT OR PHOOEY? Tony Randall and Jack Klugman both won Best Actor Emmys for TV's *The Odd Couple.*
Fact.

HOT OR NOT? Glitter Rock
Hot. Thanks to the likes of David Bowie's Ziggy Stardust, glitter was glam and rocked on in the '70s.

RAPID RECALL **Q:** What is the name of Josie and the Pussycats' cat?
A: Sebastian

ORDER UP! **A.** Martin Scorsese's off-kilter character asks himself, "You talking to me?" in *Taxi Driver.*
B. A gas shortage leads to long lines at the pumps; California initiates gas rationing on alternate days.
A. (1976) B. (1979)

HIT PARADE **Sing** a line from the O'Jays song "Love Train."

DEAD OR ALIVE? Langston Hughes (writer)
Dead. Hughes met his maker in 1967.

BLAST FROM THE PAST

19

FACT OR PHOOEY? When U.S. postal workers went on strike in 1970, no mail was delivered for almost three months.
Phooey! The U.S. Army stepped into the rescue.

HOT OR NOT? KISS
Hot. These rockers rocked on through the '70s, wearing trademark black and white makeup, platform shoes, and big hair.

RAPID RECALL **Q:** On the television show *Wonder Woman*, how did Diana change into Wonder Woman?
A: She spun around.

ORDER UP! **A.** Francis Ford Coppola releases the critically acclaimed *Apocalypse Now*.
B. The last U.S. combat troops pull out of Vietnam.
B. (1972) A. (1979)

HIT PARADE **Q:** What did singer Terry Jacks have with his seasons in the sun?
A: Joy and fun (from "Seasons in the Sun")

DEAD OR ALIVE? Jimmy Durante
Alive. Durante kept the laughter coming until 1980.

BLAST FROM THE PAST

20

FACT OR PHOOEY? Walt Disney proudly presided over the opening day festivities at Disney World in Florida.
Phooey! Walt died before Disney World was completed.

HOT OR NOT? *Upstairs, Downstairs*
Hot. This award-winning British TV comedy series about servants and their employers aired on PBS in 1973.

RAPID RECALL Q: What country was formed as a result of a civil war and the splitting of East Pakistan and West Pakistan in 1971?
A: Bangladesh

ORDER UP! **A.** The Alaska Pipeline begins pumping oil from Prudhoe Bay to the port of Valdez.
B. The U.S. Supreme Court legalizes abortion with the *Roe vs. Wade* decision.
B. (1973) A. (1977)

HIT PARADE Q: What Scott Joplin-composed instrumental peaked at number three on the charts after it was featured in *The Sting*?
A: "The Entertainer"

DEAD OR ALIVE? Truman Capote
Alive. The author of *Breakfast at Tiffany's* and *In Cold Blood* died in 1984.

BLAST FROM **THE PAST**

21

FACT OR PHOOEY? In *Grease*, the T-Birds' rivals are the Scorpions.
Fact.

HOT OR NOT? Power Dressing
Not. This trend took off in the '80s when women tried to look glam and professional with the same suit.

RAPID RECALL Ω: What two giant gifts did China give to the U.S. as a goodwill gesture in 1970?
A: Two giant pandas

ORDER UP! **A.** Dustin Hoffman and Meryl Streep square off in *Kramer vs. Kramer.*
B. Richard Dreyfus plays with his mashed potatoes in Steven Spielberg's *Close Encounters of the Third Kind.*
B. (1977) A. (1979)

HIT PARADE Ω: In what aptly titled song does Carly Simon sing, "You probably think this song is about you"?
A: "You're so Vain."

DEAD OR ALIVE? Ricky Nelson
Alive. Ozzie and Harriet's singing son died tragically in 1985.

BLAST FROM THE PAST

22

FACT OR PHOOEY? The Three Mile Island nuclear power plant incident occurred in the state of Connecticut.
Phooey! It happened in Pennsylvania.

HOT OR NOT? Barry Manilow
Hot. The songwriter, famous for being cool and un-cool at the same time, was at the height of his popularity during the 1970s.

RAPID RECALL Ω: Nike, Inc. got its start after track coach Bill Bowerman poured rubber into what kitchen appliance?
A: A waffle iron

ORDER UP! **A.** Two amateur electronics enthusiasts, Stephen Wozniak and Steven Jobs, create the Apple computer in a California garage.
B. A ceasefire ends involvement of U.S. ground troops in Vietnam.
B. (1973) A. (1976)

HIT PARADE **Sing** a line from "Tears of a Clown" or name the group that sang it.
A: Smokey Robinson and the Miracles

DEAD OR ALIVE? Woody Guthrie
Dead. Guthrie wrote more than 100 folk songs, including "This Land is Your Land," before he died in 1967.

BLAST FROM THE PAST

23

FACT OR PHOOEY? Before *Golden Girls*, Betty White had a role on *The Mary Tyler Moore Show.*
Fact.

HOT OR NOT? *Our Miss Brooks*
Not. This popular 1950s TV show starred Eve Arden.

RAPID RECALL **Q:** What magazine made Beverly Johnson the first African American cover girl of a major fashion publication?
A: *Vogue*

ORDER UP! **A.** During a sweltering heat wave, a 25-hour blackout strikes New York, sending looters on a citywide crime spree.
B. Sony introduces the Walkman® for $200.
A. (1977) B. (1979)

HIT PARADE **Q:** What singer said, "Winter, spring, summer, or fall/all you have to do is call/and I'll be there, yeah, yeah, yeah" in his 1971 single?
A: James Taylor (from "You've Got a Friend")

DEAD OR ALIVE? Roger Maris
Alive. The first man who broke Babe Ruth's record of 60 home runs in one season died in 1985.

BLAST FROM THE PAST

24

FACT OR PHOOEY? The microprocessor was introduced by Compaq in 1971.
Phooey! Intel introduced it.

HOT OR NOT? *The Mary Tyler Moore Show*
Hot. The Emmy award–winning show featured Mary and her softhearted but grouchy boss Lou Grant, played by Ed Asner.

RAPID RECALL **Q:** What is the name of the blissful dog in the comic strip *Garfield*?
A: Opie

ORDER UP! **A.** Priscilla gets $750,000 from Elvis in her divorce settlement.
B. Dan White claims Twinkies drove him to shoot San Francisco Mayor George Moscone and openly gay City Supervisor Harvey Milk.
A. (1973) B. (1979)

HIT PARADE **Q:** Name the duo behind 1975's biggest hit "Love Will Keep Us Together."
A: Captain & Tennille

DEAD OR ALIVE? Sir Laurence Olivier
Alive. The Shakespearean actor who won an Oscar for his work in *Rebecca* died in 1989.

BLAST FROM *THE* *PAST*

25

FACT OR PHOOEY? Because of the gasoline shortage, Daylight Savings Time was observed all year during 1974.
Fact.

HOT OR NOT? The Goth look
Not. Originally dating back to the 1800s, this dark look was reborn in London, but not until 1981.

RAPID RECALL Q: How much is a Susan B. Anthony coin worth?
A: One U.S. dollar

ORDER UP! **A.** Decathlon winner Bruce Jenner becomes a household name and a Wheaties® pin-up following the Montreal Summer Olympics.
B. The Sugar Hill Gang brings rap to the masses with their hit, "Rapper's Delight."
A. (1976) B. (1979)

HIT PARADE Q: Fill in the blanks in this John Denver hit: "Sunshine on my shoulders makes me happy, Sunshine in my eyes can ___ ___ ___."
A: Make me cry (from "Sunshine On My Shoulders")

DEAD OR ALIVE? Otis Redding
Dead. This "Sittin' on the Dock of the Bay" singer croaked in 1967.

BLAST FROM THE PAST

26

FACT OR PHOOEY?   Major League Baseball's first female umpire resigned a few hours after her first game.
Fact.

HOT OR NOT?   Star-studded disaster flicks
Hot. One followed another, including smash hits like *Airport, Towering Inferno,* and *The Poseidon Adventure.*

RAPID RECALL   **Q:** What company introduced LipSmackers® in 1973, featuring fabulous flavors like Dr. Pepper, Good & Plenty, and Orange Crush?
A: Bonne Bell

ORDER UP!   **A.** *Hustler* bigwig Larry Flynt is shot and paralyzed after leaving a Georgia courthouse.
B. The World Trade Center opens its first office.
B. (1972) A. (1978)

HIT PARADE   **Q:** Who sang the 1972 hit "You Are the Sunshine of My Life"?
A: Stevie Wonder

DEAD OR ALIVE?   Jack Webb
Alive. Just the facts, ma'am: *Dragnet*'s star died in 1982.

BLAST FROM THE PAST

27

FACT OR PHOOEY?   Bill Gates graduated from Harvard in 1974.
Phooey! Actually, he dropped out of Harvard during that year.

HOT OR NOT?   Rubik's Cube
Not. The colorful mind-bending puzzle was a phenomenon of the 1980s.

RAPID RECALL   **Q:** What two cities did the first regularly scheduled Concorde route fly to and from?
A: New York and Paris

ORDER UP!   **A.** The U.S. celebrates the first Earth Day.
B. The Senate committee begins Watergate hearings.
A. (1970) B. (1973)

HIT PARADE   **Q:** Paul McCartney and his new band Wings didn't see anything wrong with singing what kind of silly songs in 1976?
A: Love songs (from "Silly Love Songs")

DEAD OR ALIVE?   Helen Keller
Dead. This advocate for the deaf and blind died in 1968.

BLAST FROM THE PAST

28

FACT OR PHOOEY? The Ben & Jerry's Ice Cream company was formed in a renovated gas station in 1978.
Fact.

HOT OR NOT? *A Chorus Line*
Hot. This high-kicking production was the most successful Broadway show of the 1970s.

RAPID RECALL Q: Who portrayed The Incredible Hulk on the 1978 TV series of the same name?
A: Lou Ferrigno

ORDER UP! **A.** NBC broadcasts *Gone with the Wind* and scores record-breaking ratings.
B. *Ms.* magazine debuts with Gloria Steinem at the helm.
B. (1972) A. (1976)

HIT PARADE Q: According to Paul Simon, how many ways are there to leave your lover?
A: Fifty (from "Fifty Ways to Leave Your Lover")

DEAD OR ALIVE? John Steinbeck
Dead. *The Grapes of Wrath* author died in 1968.

29

FACT OR PHOOEY? Track and field star Mark Spitz became the first Olympian to win seven gold medals.
Phooey! Spitz is a swimmer.

HOT OR NOT? "Moonies"
Hot. This was the nickname given to cult members of the Unification Church, led by South Korean Reverend Sun Myung Moon.

RAPID RECALL Q: What is the name of the real-life cowboy who appeared as Taggart in the cast of Mel Brooks' *Blazing Saddles*?
A: Slim Pickens

ORDER UP! A. *Monday Night Football* debuts on ABC, with Howard Cosell, Frank Gifford, and Don Meredith giving pithy play-by-play.
B. Martina Navratilova mows down Chris Evert (2–6, 6–4, 7–5) on the Wimbledon green.
A. (1970) B. (1978)

HIT PARADE Q: What month and year were the Four Seasons remembering in their hit subtitled "Oh, What A Night"?
A: December 1963

DEAD OR ALIVE? William Holden
Alive. The *Stalag 17* and *Sabrina* actor died in 1981.

BLAST FROM THE PAST

30

FACT OR PHOOEY?　The original price tag on an Apple I Computer was $666.66.
Fact.

HOT OR NOT?　Hula Hoops
Not. Inspired by an Australian toy, Hula Hoops had their heyday in the '50s.

RAPID RECALL　**Q:** What 1975 Steven Spielberg thriller kept audiences out of the water?
A: *Jaws*

ORDER UP!　**A.** Loni Anderson turns heads in *WKRP In Cincinnati.*
B. An Operation Baby Lift plane crashes, killing nearly 200 Vietnamese orphans and humanitarian aid workers.
B. (1975) A. (1978)

HIT PARADE　**Sing** two lines from "Don't Go Breaking My Heart" or name the woman Elton John teamed up with to record it.
A: Kiki Dee

DEAD OR ALIVE?　Peter Sellers
Alive. The Pink Panther passed away in 1980.

31

FACT OR PHOOEY? The Beatles broke up in 1970.
Fact.

HOT OR NOT? Boxer shorts
Not. Briefs didn't come down in popularity until the 1980s, when the boxer took over.

RAPID RECALL **Q:** Which famous pop singer appeared on the '70s sitcoms *Good Times* and *Diff'rent Strokes*?
A: Janet Jackson

ORDER UP! **A.** Helen Reddy's "I Am Woman" roars on the radio.
B. Alex Haley publishes the epic novel *Roots*.
A. (1972) B. (1976)

HIT PARADE **Q:** Who sang the ironically titled "I Write the Songs," written by Bruce Johnson.
A: Barry Manilow

DEAD OR ALIVE? Carl Jung
Dead. The Swedish founder of analytical psychology and former friend of Freud died in 1961.

BLAST FROM THE PAST

32

FACT OR PHOOEY? Cigarette ads were banned on radio and TV by 1971.
Fact.

HOT OR NOT? The Romantic look
Hot. 1970s rockers got Romantic with lace, velvet, and ruffles.

RAPID RECALL **Q:** What is the name of the politically based and often controversial '70s show starring Bea Arthur?
A: *Maude*

ORDER UP! **A.** Cops nab postal worker and "Son Of Sam" killer David Berkowitz in New York.
B. Bill Gates starts Microsoft with childhood chum Paul Allen.
B. (1975) A. (1977)

HIT PARADE **Sing** a line from ABBA's "Dancing Queen" or name the country this super group called home.
A: Sweden

DEAD OR ALIVE? Henry Fonda
Alive. Jane's dad died in 1982, shortly after his highly acclaimed role in *On Golden Pond*.

BLAST FROM THE PAST

33

FACT OR PHOOEY? The Wang 1200 was a popular disco dance, similar to the Hustle.
Phooey! It was the first word processor.

HOT OR NOT? *Monty Python's Flying Circus*
Hot. This British comedy show first aired in the U.S. in the early '70s and had Yanks laughing their bums off.

RAPID RECALL **Q:** What name falls between "*Jonathan*" and "*Seagull*" in Richard Bach's popular novel about a stubborn bird?
A: *Livingston*

ORDER UP! **A.** Beer-bellied beer drinkers find hope in a bottle when Miller debuts "Lite," the first low-calorie beer.
B. The first New York City Marathon is run, attracting 126 starters. The entire twenty-six mile course is in Central Park.
B. (1970) A. (1975)

HIT PARADE **Q:** Where was Jimmy Buffet wasting away again?
A: In Margaritaville

DEAD OR ALIVE? Rock Hudson
Alive. Hudson's AIDS-related death surprised the public, but he didn't die until1985.

BLAST FROM THE PAST

34

FACT OR PHOOEY? Evel Knievel coined the phrase, "Kids, do not try this at home."
Fact.

HOT OR NOT? Brylcreem
Not. The popularity of the Fab Four's "long" loose locks pushed Brylcreem to the unfashionable side in the 1960s.

RAPID RECALL **Q:** "Things a policeman might say" or "Things found at a supermarket" could be subjects found in what '70s game show?
A: $10,000 Pyramid (also $25,000 Pyramid)

ORDER UP! **A.** Facing impeachment, President Nixon resigns from office.
B. In an unsuccessful bid for peace, Britain takes over direct rule of Northern Ireland.
B. (1972) A. (1974)

HIT PARADE **Q:** Name two of the Bee Gee's three 1978 number one hits.
A: "Staying Alive," "Night Fever," "How Deep is Your Love?"

DEAD OR ALIVE? Jack Kerouac
Dead. This famous Beat writer turned up his toes in 1969.

BLAST FROM **THE PAST**

35

FACT OR PHOOEY? After being exiled, the Ayatollah Khomeini returned to Iran in 1979.
Fact.

HOT OR NOT? *Up The Down Staircase*
Not. Bel Kaufman's novel was on the best-seller list in 1965.

RAPID RECALL **Q:** In which '70s game show did amateur contestants showcase their talents in the hopes of getting scored by celebrity judges?
A: *The Gong Show*

ORDER UP! **A.** North and South Vietnam unite, Hanoi becomes the capital city, and Saigon is renamed Ho Chi Minh City.
B. 18-year-olds head to the polls after the 26th Amendment to the U.S. Constitution is passed lowering the voting age.
B. (1971) A. (1976)

HIT PARADE **Q:** What singer had a hit with "Lay Down Sally"?
A: Eric Clapton

DEAD OR ALIVE? Judy Garland
Dead. *The Wizard of Oz*'s Dorothy died in 1969.

BLAST FROM THE PAST

36

FACT OR PHOOEY? In the mid-70s, Trident® gum ads featured a goofy multi-colored cartoon zebra.
Phooey! Fruit Stripe Gum® featured the zebra.

HOT OR NOT? Whip Inflation Now (WIN)
Hot. This short-lived and unsuccessful campaign to curb inflation was led by President Ford.

RAPID RECALL **Q:** Which *Scooby-Doo* character wears glasses?
A: Velma

ORDER UP! **A.** George Carlin hosts the first episode of *Saturday Night Live*.
B. Billie Jean King defeats Bobby Riggs in the "Battle of the Sexes" tennis match.
B. (1973) A. (1975)

HIT PARADE **Q:** Frankie Valli had a comeback with the theme song from what movie that celebrated the decade of his first heyday?
A: *Grease*

DEAD OR ALIVE? Ernest Hemingway
Dead. "Papa" lost his will to live in 1961.

37

FACT OR PHOOEY?	The original Benji, a dog named Higgins, also starred as the mutt on TV's *Petticoat Junction*. Fact.
HOT OR NOT?	Padded shoulders Not. Women's fashions featured the allure of the quarterback during the 1980s.
RAPID RECALL	**Q:** What 1977 Woody Allen movie inspired a fashion trend that saw women wearing men's clothing? A: *Annie Hall*
ORDER UP!	**A.** Rock icon Janis Joplin dies at age 27. **B.** President Carter officially pardons all draft dodgers, permitting those who fled the country safe return. A. (1970) B. (1977)
HIT PARADE	**Put on your dancing shoes** and imitate John Travolta in *Saturday Night Fever*.
DEAD OR ALIVE?	L. Ron Hubbard Alive. The founder of the Church of Scientology and author of *Dianetics* died in 1986.

BLAST FROM THE PAST

38

FACT OR PHOOEY? The *Garfield* cartoon strip went into syndication in 1978.
Fact. Cartoonist Jim Davis started the Garfield craze.

HOT OR NOT? Puffball skirts
Not. The cloud-like skirts were popular with prom-goers in the 1980s.

RAPID RECALL **Q:** What 1971 Stanley Kubrick cult classic was criticized for its disturbing violence and sex scenes?
A: *A Clockwork Orange*

ORDER UP! **A.** National Guardsmen shoot and kill four student demonstrators at Ohio's Kent State University.
B. *The Jeffersons* move on up "to a deluxe apartment in the sky"—and a primetime spot on CBS.
A. (1970) B. (1975)

HIT PARADE **Q:** What did M have everyone talking about in 1979?
A: Pop Muzik

DEAD OR ALIVE? Winston Churchill
Dead. The British Prime Minister who coined the term "Iron Curtain" died in 1965.

BLAST FROM **THE PAST**

39

FACT OR PHOOEY? Walter Matthau played the role of Morris Buttermaker in only two of the three *Bad News Bears* movies.
Phooey! Matthau starred in all three.

HOT OR NOT? Adidas shoes
Not. Rappers Run D.M.C. made these runners popular during the 1980s—without laces, of course.

RAPID RECALL **Q:** What is the name of the diner where much of the movie *American Graffitti* takes place?
A: Mel's Diner

ORDER UP! **A.** Gerald Ford is sworn in as president and declares that "the long nightmare is over."
B. South African activist Steve Biko dies in police custody.
A. (1974) B. (1977)

HIT PARADE **Sing** a line from the Coca-Cola jingle that became a Top 10 hit in 1971.(A: "I'd Like to Teach the World to Sing" or "I'd Like to Buy The World a Coke")

DEAD OR ALIVE? Lillian Gish
Alive. Born in 1893, the silent screen's first lady lived until 1993.

BLAST FROM THE PAST

40

FACT OR PHOOEY? Introduced in 1978, Speak & Spell used new-fangled technology to create convincing speech sounds.
Fact.

HOT OR NOT? *Land of the Lost*
Hot. This Sid and Marty Krofft creation premiered in 1974 and was a Tyrannosaurus-sized Saturday morning hit.

RAPID RECALL Q: In 1979, mischievous magpies Heckle and Jeckle shared billing with what famous mouse in their animated TV series?
A: Mighty Mouse (in *The New Adventures of Mighty Mouse and Heckle and Jeckle*)

ORDER UP! A. Margaret Thatcher becomes the first female British Prime Minister.
B. The Symbionese Liberation Army kidnaps Patty Hearst.
B. (1974) A. (1979)

HIT PARADE Q: What country crooner had a crossover hit with 1975's "Rhinestone Cowboy"?
A: Glen Campbell

DEAD OR ALIVE? Greta Garbo
Alive. The screen legend died alone in 1990 at the age of 84.

41

FACT OR PHOOEY? Hockey great Mario Lemieux invented the table game Air Hockey in 1972.
Phooey! Bob Lemieux (no relation) created this popular table game.

HOT OR NOT? *The Exorcist*
Hot. Linda Blair turned heads in this 1973 creepy cult classic.

RAPID RECALL **Q:** Complete this quote from ABC's 1970s Health and Nutrition series: "I Hanker for a Hunka _____."
A: Cheese

ORDER UP! **A.** Teamster boss Jimmy Hoffa mysteriously disappears.
B. Tom Wopat and John Schneider are hick heartthrobs in *The Dukes of Hazzard*.
A. (1975) B. (1979)

HIT PARADE **Q:** Fill in the blanks from this 1979 Bob Seger song "Don't try and take me to a disco, you'll never even get me out on ____ ____."
A: the floor (from "Old Time Rock and Roll")

DEAD OR ALIVE? Lenny Bruce
Dead. The stand-up comedian died in 1966.

BLAST FROM THE PAST

42

FACT OR PHOOEY? On *H. R. Pufnstuf*, Jimmy called his magic flute Felix.
Phooey! Jimmy's flute was named Freddie.

HOT OR NOT? *The Adventures of Ozzie and Harriet*
Not. America's favorite family left their sitcom life behind in 1966 after 14 years in prime time and an astonishing 435 episodes.

RAPID RECALL **Q:** What Olympian made the "wedge" a sassy and stylish haircut in the 1970s?
A: Dorothy Hamill

ORDER UP! **A.** Olivia Newton-John and John Travolta sizzle at the box office in *Grease*.
B. Premier Russian dancer Mikhail Baryshnikov defects and joins the American Ballet Theatre.
B. (1974) A. (1978)

HIT PARADE **Q:** What disco diva sang the hit "Hot Stuff"?
A: Donna Summer

DEAD OR ALIVE? J. Robert Oppenheimer (scientist)
Dead. The "Father of the Atomic Bomb" bought the farm in 1967.

BLAST FROM THE PAST

43

FACT OR PHOOEY? There were 12 mouseketeers in *The New Mickey Mouse Club*.
Fact. (But no Jimmy, Dodd, Cubby, or Annette . . .)

HOT OR NOT? The Mashed Potato
Not. The early 1960s song created a dance craze and was followed by another hit entitled "Gravy (For My Mashed Potatoes)".

RAPID RECALL **Q:** Under what record label did the Jackson 5 record under?
A: Motown Records

ORDER UP! **A.** The U.S. and Iran sign a $10 billion arms sale deal.
B. Ford grants a "full, free, and absolute pardon" to ex-President Nixon.
B. (1974) A. (1976)

HIT PARADE **Sing** a line from Lynyrd Skynyrd's musical tribute to a southern state.
A: "Sweet Home Alabama"

DEAD OR ALIVE? Fred Astaire
Alive. Ginger Rogers's dance partner died in 1987.

BLAST FROM THE PAST

44

FACT OR PHOOEY? 1971's *The Andromeda Strain* was based on a book written by Michael Crichton.
Fact.

HOT OR NOT? Evel Knievel
Hot. Though he started doing his wild stunts during the late '60s, the rise and fall of his popularity occurred during the 1970s.

RAPID RECALL **Q:** What 1978 movie musical was based on a L. Frank Baum novel?
A: *The Wiz*

ORDER UP! **A.** Woodward and Bernstein publish *All the President's Men*, detailing Nixon's political demise.
B. Congress creates the Environmental Protection Agency, and Nixon signs the Clean Air Act.
B. (1970) A. (1974)

HIT PARADE **Q:** What group's 1976 album went to number one and featured hits like "Go Your Own Way" and "Don't Stop"?
A: Fleetwood Mac

DEAD OR ALIVE? Natalie Wood
Alive. It was not until 1981 that the 43-year-old actress drowned tragically off the coast of California.

BLAST FROM THE PAST

45

FACT OR PHOOEY? Founded in 1974, LeSportSac made thermal sleeping bags out of parachute nylon.
Phooey! LeSportSac made nylon duffle bags.

HOT OR NOT? Loon pants
Hot. These unisex trousers weren't the most flattering look, but then again, it was the '70s.

RAPID RECALL **Q:** What is the object in the video game Frogger?
A: To hop to the other side

ORDER UP! **A.** Upstate New York's Love Canal residents evacuate their homes.
B. Stephen King raises the payback bar in his first novel, *Carrie*.
B. (1974) A. (1979)

HIT PARADE **Q:** Name the 1975 Queen rock-opera anthem resurrected by Wayne and Garth in the 1992 movie *Wayne's World*.
A: "Bohemian Rhapsody"

DEAD OR ALIVE? Dwight D. Eisenhower
Dead. The 34th President of the United States, also known as Ike, passed away in 1969.

BLAST FROM THE PAST

46

FACT OR PHOOEY? Sears Roebuck and Co. helped bankroll *Soul Train* in exchange for the rights to use the show to promote a line of tube tops.
Phooey! Sears used *Soul Train* to promote a line of record players.

HOT OR NOT? *Charlie's Angels*
Hot. Farrah Fawcett, Kate Jackson, and Jaclyn Smith played the original trio of sexy PIs.

RAPID RECALL **Q:** What shoemaker had a sweet success with the debut of the stiletto (or disco) slide in 1978?
A: Candies

ORDER UP! **A.** *M*A*S*H* begins a long tour of duty on CBS.
B. Soviet troops invade Afghanistan, stirring world protests.
A. (1972) B. (1979)

HIT PARADE **Sing** a line from John Denver's "Thank God I'm a Country Boy."

DEAD OR ALIVE? Ethel Merman
Alive. "The Queen of Broadway" died in 1984.

BLAST FROM THE PAST

47

FACT OR PHOOEY? Nolan Bushnell, the creator of Pong and Atari, launched the Chuck E. Cheese franchise in the late '70s.
Fact. Bushnell opened the first Chuck E. Cheese Pizza Time Theater in 1977.

HOT OR NOT? Sonny and Cher
Hot. *The Sonny and Cher Show* made variety the spice of '70s TV life.

RAPID RECALL **Q:** What brand helped kids of the '70s avoid fashion faux-paws with their line of animal kingdom coded separates, made to mix and match?
A: Garanimals

ORDER UP! **A.** The U.S. and Panama sign a treaty that relinquishes control of the canal to Panama by the year 2000.
B. PBS airs *An American Family*, a series documenting the lives of the dysfunctional Loud family.
B. (1973) A. (1977)

HIT PARADE **Q:** Who sang "Hotel California"?
A: The Eagles

DEAD OR ALIVE? Douglas MacArthur
Dead. This five-star general gave his final salute in 1964.

BLAST FROM THE PAST

48

FACT OR PHOOEY? The popular and portable electronic game Simon, released in 1978, was named after the classic kids' game "Simon Says."
Fact.

HOT OR NOT? David Cassidy
Hot. He was a major teen heartthrob during his *Partridge Family* days, from 1970 to 1974, singing "I Think I Love You" and other pop hits.

RAPID RECALL Q: What surfwear clothing line sported two bare feet on its logo and became a must-have item in the '70s?
A: Hang Ten

ORDER UP! A. A U.N. Security Council resolution calls for an independent Palestinian state.
B. Syria and Egypt attack Israel on Yom Kippur.
B. (1973) A. (1976)

HIT PARADE Q: What did K.C. and the Sunshine Band invite people to shake, shake, shake?
A: Your booty (from "(Shake, Shake, Shake) Shake Your Booty")

DEAD OR ALIVE? David O. Selznick (Hollywood producer)
Dead. This *Gone with the Wind* producer gave up the ghost in 1965.

BLAST FROM THE PAST

49

FACT OR PHOOEY?   Wayne Gretzky entered the National Hockey League in 1979.
Fact.

HOT OR NOT?   Merry Pranksters
Not. This was the name of author Ken Kesey's group of psychedelic friends who were well known in the 1960s.

RAPID RECALL   **Q:** What hairstyle trend did Bo "Perfect 10" Derek inspire in 1979?
A: Cornrow braids

ORDER UP!   **A.** President Nixon makes an unprecedented eight-day visit to China and meets with Mao Zedong.
B. The U.S. severs formal ties with Taiwan and establishes diplomatic relations with China.
A. (1972) B. (1979)

HIT PARADE   **Q:** In a 1973 release, who asks the piano man to sing us a song?
A: Billy Joel (from "Piano Man")

DEAD OR ALIVE?   Dorothy Dandridge
Dead. The *Carmen Jones* actress that Halle Berry portrayed in an HBO movie died in 1965.

BLAST FROM THE PAST

50

FACT OR PHOOEY? Mr. Ricardo was Tattoo's boss on *Fantasy Island*.
Phooey! Mr. Roarke, played by Ricardo Montalban, was the island's head honcho.

HOT OR NOT? The Watusi
Not. They were doing the Watusi way back in 1964.

RAPID RECALL **Q:** What company made and sold Toughskins, the rugged and fashionably funky jeans popular with both kids and moms in the 1970s?
A: Sears Roebuck and Co.

ORDER UP! **A.** The House votes 410–4 to investigate President Nixon.
B. Henry Kissinger secretly negotiates with the North Vietnamese in Paris.
B. (1972) A. (1974)

HIT PARADE **Q:** What is the title of the Carpenter's first number one hit?
A: "Close to You"

DEAD OR ALIVE? Ian Fleming (author)
Dead. This James Bond and *Chitty Chitty Bang Bang* creator died in 1964.

BLAST FROM **THE** PAST

51

FACT OR PHOOEY? Hacky Sack was invented by President Carter's daughter, Amy, in 1972.
Phooey! Mike Marshall created Hacky Sack while he was recovering from a knee injury.

HOT OR NOT? *The Addams Family*
Not. You rang? The creepy and kooky TV family was on the air from 1964 to 1966.

RAPID RECALL **Q:** What plastic toy introduced in 1974 magically—and marvelously—shrunk when you baked it?
A: Shrinky Dinks

ORDER UP! **A.** The young Mia Farrow graces the first *People* magazine cover.
B. Sylvester Stallone busts on to the scene in *Rocky*.
A. (1974) B. (1976)

HIT PARADE **Q:** According to Peter, Paul, and Mary, what did Puff the Magic Dragon frolic in?
A: The autumn mist (from "Puff the Magic Dragon")

DEAD OR ALIVE? Aunt Jemima
Dead. The pancake syrup lady, whose real name was Rosie Riles, died in 1969.

BLAST FROM THE PAST

52

FACT OR PHOOEY? Race car driver Mario Andretti won the Indianapolis 500 for a record fourth time in 1977.
Phooey! It was A. J. Foyt who earned this distinction in 1977.

HOT OR NOT? *I Spy*
Not. From 1965–1968, Bill Cosby and Robert Culp played undercover secret agents posing as a tennis player and his trainer.

RAPID RECALL **Q:** What was the popular slang term for one's C.B. radio pseudonym?
A: Handle

ORDER UP! **A.** Sony introduces the Betamax.
B. Jim Morrison tragically breaks on through to the other side and is found dead at age 27.
B. (1971) A. (1975)

HIT PARADE **Q:** What are the first two words of the theme song from TV's *Laverne & Shirley*?
A: Schalemiel, schlamazel

DEAD OR ALIVE? Stan Laurel
Dead. Oh Ollie, Stan died in 1965.

BLAST FROM THE PAST

53

FACT OR PHOOEY? The Mediterranean fruit bat threatened California crops in 1975.
Phooey! The fruit fly threatened California crops in 1975.

HOT OR NOT? Bread
Hot. Bread rose to fame in the 1970s with songs like "Baby I'm-A Want You" and "It Don't Matter to Me."

RAPID RECALL Q: "Voulez-vous couchez avec moi ce soir?" became a popular catchphrase in the mid-70s due to what Patti LaBelle song?
A: "Lady Marmalade"

ORDER UP! **A.** Congress passes the Freedom of Information Act over President Ford's veto.
B. Sally Field is *Norma Rae* at the movies.
A. (1974) B. (1979)

HIT PARADE **Sing** a line from the *Three's Company* theme song.

DEAD OR ALIVE? Butterfly McQueen
Alive. *Gone with the Wind*'s Prissy died in 1995.

BLAST FROM THE PAST

54

FACT OR PHOOEY?   In 1971, the UN declared that there were 576,100 tons of tea in Boston, Massachusetts.
Phooey! The UN declared there was 576,100 tons of tea in China.

HOT OR NOT?   Blaxploitation films
Hot. Hip dialogue, sexy characters, and messages of black power made this controversial genre a hit with African American audiences in the '70s.

RAPID RECALL   **Q:** What 1970s CBS family drama chronicled a family of ten living in rural Virginia during the Great Depression?
A: *The Waltons*

ORDER UP!   **A.** Unemployment reaches 8.9%, the highest level since 1941.
B. Erica Jong titillates readers with her first novel, *Fear of Flying.*
B. (1973) A. (1975)

HIT PARADE   **Q:** What New Wave rockers released "Rock Lobster" in 1979 and topped the pop charts with "Love Shack" ten years later?
A: The B-52s

DEAD OR ALIVE?   Vivien Leigh
Dead. The actress who played Scarlett O'Hara and Blanche DuBois died in 1967.

55

FACT OR PHOOEY? Kevin Bacon's first credited screen appearance was in 1978's *Animal House.*
Fact. This first National Lampoon flick remains a crude—but classic—parody of college life.

HOT OR NOT? *All in the Family*
Hot. Those were the days—Archie Bunker called his wife Dingbat and his son-in-law Meathead on this hugely popular TV show.

RAPID RECALL **Q:** Were trousers typically worn tight or loose in the '70s?
A: Tight

ORDER UP! **A.** Bobby Fischer becomes the first American to win the World Chess Championship.
B. Oscar® goes mad for *One Flew Over the Cuckoo's Nest,* awarding the film Best Picture, Director, Actor, and Actress.
A. (1972) B. (1975)

HIT PARADE **Q:** In 1975, what was the major album release from the New Jersey native hailed as "The New Bob Dylan"?
A: *Born To Run* (by Bruce Springsteen)

DEAD OR ALIVE? Rocky Marciano (professional boxer)
Dead. The legendary boxer died in 1969.

56

FACT OR PHOOEY? In 1977, the makers of Stretch Armstrong released Stretch Stallone, modeled after *Rocky* star Slyvester Stallone.
Phooey! They released Stretch Monster, Armstrong's evil green-fanged foe.

HOT OR NOT? Mikhail Baryshnikov
Hot. His name was synonymous with ballet during the 1970s.

RAPID RECALL **Q:** In *Escape to Witch Mountain,* what supernatural power does Tia hold?
A: She can see into the future (clairvoyance)

ORDER UP! **A.** The new 55 mile-per-hour speed limit forces Mario Andretti wannabes to hit the brakes.
B. John Irving comes out with *The World According to Garp.*
A. (1974) B. (1978)

HIT PARADE **Sing** a line from the Doobie Brothers ultra-catchy tune "Black Water."

DEAD OR ALIVE? Raymond Burr
Alive. The star of the popular *Perry Mason* TV series died in 1993.

BLAST FROM THE PAST

57

FACT OR PHOOEY? Robert Redford and Paul Newman teamed up to make 1975's *Three Days of the Condor*.
Phooey! The film's got Redford, but no Newman.

HOT OR NOT? The baby doll look
Not. First hot in the 1950s as sleep wear, it returned with the grunge look of the 1990s.

RAPID RECALL **Q:** In what 1978 Beatles-inspired rock musical did the Bee Gees appear?
A: *Sgt. Pepper's Lonely Hearts Club Band*

ORDER UP! **A.** Chicago's Sears Tower opens as the tallest building in the world.
B. *All Things Considered* debuts on National Public Radio.
B. (1971) A. (1973)

HIT PARADE **Q:** What rock giant released *Bat Out of Hell* in 1978?
A: Meat Loaf

DEAD OR ALIVE? Andy Warhol
Alive. Pop art's papa didn't die until 1987.

1980s

1

FACT OR PHOOEY? The number of Barbie® dolls surpassed the American population in 1985.
Fact.

HOT OR NOT? Boom boxes
Hot. The bigger the better was the rule with these musical status symbols in the '80s. After all, what good was a boom box if it couldn't handle the bass?

RAPID RECALL Q: Who wrote the poem "somewhere i have never travelled, gladly beyond," quoted in Woody Allen's 1986 film *Hannah and Her Sisters*?
A: e.e. cummings

ORDER UP! **A.** *Cats* begins its run as Broadway's longest-running play. MeOow!
B. After 28 years, the Berlin Wall opens to the West; thousands gather to celebrate and pocket chunks of the historic concrete.
A. (1982) B. (1989)

HIT PARADE **Sing** a line from Peter Gabriel's "In Your Eyes."

DEAD OR ALIVE? Freddie Mercury
Alive. Queen's leading man lived until 1991.

BLAST FROM THE PAST

2

FACT OR PHOOEY? *Magnum P.I.* was set on Southern California's Catalina island.
Phooey! The series was set (and shot) on Hawaii's most popular island, Oahu.

HOT OR NOT? Vanilla Ice
Not. "Ice Ice Baby" didn't chill at the top of the charts until 1990.

RAPID RECALL **Q:** What designer took a swan dive into the apparel market with her own line of jeans in the 1980s?
A: Gloria Vanderbilt

ORDER UP! **A.** Yuri V. Andropov succeeds the late Leonid I. Brezhnev as leader of the Soviet Union.
B. The senate rejects U.S. Supreme Court Justice nominee Robert H. Bork.
A. (1982) B. (1987)

HIT PARADE **Sing** a line from one of the two 1980s movie theme songs sung by Irene Cara.
A: *Fame* ("Fame") or *Flashdance* ("What a Feeling")

DEAD OR ALIVE? Sammy Davis, Jr.
Alive. This legendary Las Vegas showman and Rat Pack member kept at it until his death in 1990.

BLAST FROM THE PAST

3

FACT OR PHOOEY? In the 1984 movie *Splash,* Daryl Hannah's character, Madison the mermaid, learns English from a New York hot dog vendor.
Phooey! Madison learns English by watching TV in a New York City department store.

HOT OR NOT? Leg warmers
Hot. It didn't matter if you were actually working out or not, leg warmers were the ultimate '80s fashion statement.

RAPID RECALL **Q:** In the *Flashdance* movie poster, which of Jennifer Beals' shoulders is bare: left or right?
A: Left

ORDER UP! **A.** President Carter breaks diplomatic ties with Iran.
B. The Reagan administration is charged with lying to Congress about the Iran-Contra scandal.
A. (1981) B. (1987)

HIT PARADE **Q:** Fill in the blanks in this 1980 Billy Joel hit: "Everybody's talking bout the ___ _____, funny but it's still ____ ___ ____ to me.
A: New sound; rock and roll (from "It's Still Rock and Roll To Me")

DEAD OR ALIVE? Greta Garbo
Alive. Hollywood's elusive leading lady didn't give up the ghost until 1990.

BLAST FROM THE PAST

4

FACT OR PHOOEY? On the ten-gallon-sized hit series *Dallas*, Sue Ellen shoots J. R. Ewing in one of the show's most talked about episodes.
Phooey! Sue Ellen's scorned sister, Kristin, did it.

HOT OR NOT? Billy Beer.
Not. Presidential brother Billy didn't have much clout for marketing his favorite brew once Jimmy Carter was voted out of office in 1980.

RAPID RECALL **Q:** Members of the rap group Run DMC hailed from what U.S. city?
A: New York

ORDER UP! **A.** President Bush holds up a pound of crack on live TV and declares a war on drugs.
B. Newly appointed Soviet leader Mikhail Gorbachev promises political and economic reform with *glasnost* and *perestroika*.
B. (1985) A. (1989)

HIT PARADE **Sing** a line from the *Beverly Hills Cop* song performed by Glen Frey.
A: "The Heat is On"

DEAD OR ALIVE? Theodore Geisel (Dr. Seuss)
Alive. The whimsical writer and illustrator continued to write and publish new works until his death in 1991.

BLAST FROM THE PAST

5

FACT OR PHOOEY? Bruce Willis did a stint as a handyman on *The Facts of Life* before getting his break as David Addison in *Moonlighting.*
Phooey! George Clooney appeared in the show's seventh season as the handsome—and handy—hunk who rebuilds Mrs. Garrett's shop.

HOT OR NOT? The Smurfs
Hot. The little blue creatures were smurftasticly popular. Their Saturday morning adventures aired from 1981–89.

RAPID RECALL **Q:** In the 1989 movie *Steel Magnolias,* what were Shelby's wedding colors?
A: Blush and bashful

ORDER UP! **A.** Spike Lee calls race relations into question in *Do the Right Thing.*
B. Fox, a new television network, takes on the big three, debuting with just ten hours of prime-time programming.
B. (1986) A. (1989)

HIT PARADE **Q:** What phone number did Tommy Tutone call looking for Jenny?
A: 867-5309 (from "867-5309/Jenny")

DEAD OR ALIVE? Ava Gardner (actress)
Alive. Frank Sinatra's famous ex died in 1990.

BLAST FROM THE PAST

6

FACT OR PHOOEY? Michael Jackson's hair caught on fire while he was filming a Coca-Cola® commercial in 1984.
Phooey! The gloved one was filming a Pepsi® commercial when the accident occurred.

HOT OR NOT? Mark Spitz
Not. Mark Spitz's glorious summer of swimming earned him seven Olympic Gold medals in 1972.

RAPID RECALL Q: What '80s hairstyle comes to life after hair is braided tightly while wet and then undone when dry?
A: Crimped

ORDER UP! A. Brainy English bloke Tim Berners-Lee develops the first World Wide Web server and browser.
B. The House votes to reject the Reagan administration's Star Wars policy.
B. (1986) A. (1989)

HIT PARADE Q: What was the first video played on MTV?
A: "Video Killed the Radio Star" (by the Buggles)

DEAD OR ALIVE? Louis Armstrong (Jazz musician)
Dead. The New Orleans horn player and music legend died in 1971.

BLAST FROM
THE **PAST**

FACT OR PHOOEY? The Running Man was a trendy 1980s cocktail.
Phooey! The Running Man was a popular mid-to-late-80s dance.

HOT OR NOT? Care Bears
Hot. A greeting card creation, the lovable bears evolved into a
licensing legacy—all without forgetting the importance of a good hug.

RAPID RECALL **Q:** What is the brand name for the popular fake plastic nails that
graced girls' hands in the 1980s?
A: Lee Press-On Nails®

ORDER UP! **A.** More than 125 million people stay home to watch the last
episode of *M*A*S*H*.
B. The U.S. congress imposes economic sanctions on South Africa,
overriding President Reagan's veto.
A. (1983) B. (1986)

HIT PARADE **Sing** a line from John Cougar Mellencamp's 1982 hit "Jack and
Diane."

DEAD OR ALIVE? Nelson Rockefeller
Dead. The former U.S. vice president and grandson of John D.
Rockefeller died in 1979.

BLAST FROM THE PAST

8

FACT OR PHOOEY? Barbara and Julie were the daughters on the 1980s sitcom *Too Close for Comfort.*
Phooey! Barbara and Julie were Ann Romano's daughters on *One Day at a Time.*

HOT OR NOT? Susan B. Anthony dollars
Not. The first U.S. currency to feature a woman was put out of circulation by the U.S. Mint in 1981.

RAPID RECALL **Q:** In the '80s TV hit *Knight Rider,* does the talking car K.I.T.T. have a male or female voice?
A: Male

ORDER UP! **A.** Apple presents the user-friendly Macintosh personal computer.
B. Visionary Jaron Lanier coins the term "virtual reality" and designs the equipment to experience it.
A. (1984) B. (1989)

HIT PARADE **Q:** In 1983, Men at Work were asking everyone if they came from where?
A: The land down under (from "Down Under")

DEAD OR ALIVE? Burl Ives (actor)
Alive. *Cat on a Hot Tin Roof*'s Big Daddy passed away in 1995.

BLAST FROM THE PAST

9

FACT OR PHOOEY? *Family Ties'* Alex P. Keaton idolized Henry Kissinger.
Phooey! Alex idolized Richard Nixon.

HOT OR NOT? Izod
Hot. The fastest way to prove yourself an upwardly mobile preppie was the little green reptile patch and upturned collar of an Izod polo.

RAPID RECALL **Q:** On what famous French play was the 1987 film *Roxanne* based?
A: *Cyrano de Bergerac* (written in 1897)

ORDER UP! **A.** Pop artist and icon Andy Warhol passes away.
B. Islamic extremists assassinate Egyptian president Anwar al-Sadat during a military parade in Cairo.
B. (1981) A. (1987)

HIT PARADE **Q:** Fill in the blanks in this Survivor-sung theme from *Rocky II:* "Went the distance now I'm back on my feet, just a man and his ____ __ _____."
A: Will to survive (from "Eye of the Tiger")

DEAD OR ALIVE? Ed Sullivan (variety show TV host)
Dead. The host with the most died in 1974.

BLAST FROM THE PAST

10

FACT OR PHOOEY? In the 1980s, bowhead was a derogatory term used to describe preppie girls, who often wore big bows in their hair.
Fact.

HOT OR NOT? *Studs*
Not. This hormone parade/dating show didn't debut until 1994. Chuck Woolery and *Love Connection* helped hook people up in the '80s.

RAPID RECALL **Q:** Valley girls (and guys) are said to have originated from what California region?
A: The San Fernando Valley

ORDER UP! **A.** Comedian John Belushi dies of a drug overdose at age 33 at Hollywood's swank Hotel Chateau Marmont.
B. Depression hits the heartland, forcing the sale or foreclosure of more than 60,000 U.S. farms.
A. (1982) B. (1986)

HIT PARADE **Q:** Fill in the blank from this Tina Turner hit: "What good's a heart when a heart ___ ___ _____."
A: Can be broken (from "What's Love Got to Do With It?")

DEAD OR ALIVE? Rod Serling (of *The Twilight Zone* fame)
Dead. *The Twilight Zone*'s host and scriptwriter passed into the great unknown in 1975.

BLAST FROM THE PAST

11

FACT OR PHOOEY? The Chicago Bears recorded "The Super Bowl Shuffle" and released a music video in 1985.
Fact.

HOT OR NOT? Abs exercisers and bun firmers.
Not. Sales of gizmos and gadgets didn't get pumping till the '90s.

RAPID RECALL Q: What sexy star appeared on the short-lived '80s teen sitcom *Square Pegs*?
A: Sarah Jessica Parker

ORDER UP! **A.** After nearly two years in Iranian captivity, 52 American hostages come home.
B. Hours after signing with the Boston Celtics, 22-year-old basketball star Len Bias dies of a drug overdose.
A. (1981) B. (1986)

HIT PARADE Q: Name the Cyndi Lauper song that contains the line, "Lying in my bed, I hear the clock tick and think of you."
A: "Time After Time"

DEAD OR ALIVE? Spiro T. Agnew
Alive. The former U.S. vice president died in 1996.

BLAST FROM THE PAST

12

FACT OR PHOOEY? Pop group Bow Wow Wow gave Boy George the boot before he found fame and fortune with the Culture Club.
Fact.

HOT OR NOT? Adoptable toys
Hot. '80s favorites like Cabbage Patch Kids® and Pound Puppies® came with papers, making them officially yours to love and hug without the hassle of walks, feeding, or bathing.

RAPID RECALL Ω: Who played the beautiful Buttercup in the 1987 movie version of *The Princess Bride*?
A: Robin Wright

ORDER UP! **A.** *Gandhi* wins the Oscar® for best picture.
B. The Dalai Lama earns the Nobel Peace Prize.
A. (1982) B. (1989)

HIT PARADE **Sing** a line from the Police song about obsession that was the number one song of 1983.
A: "Every Breath You Take"

DEAD OR ALIVE? Jean Renoir (French director)
Dead. *Le finis* for France's esteemed filmmaker came in 1979.

BLAST FROM **THE PAST**

13

FACT OR PHOOEY? In his "Dancing in the Dark" video, Bruce Springsteen picks a future *Friends'* cast member as a dance partner.
Fact. Bruce chose Courteney Cox-Arquette out of the crowd.

HOT OR NOT? Valley Girls
Hot. Oh my gawd! Unless you're like from another planet or something, you'd know that Valley Girls totally ruled in the '80s, ok?

RAPID RECALL **Q:** In the early '80s arcade game of the same name, what color is Q*bert?
A: Orange

ORDER UP! **A.** 52-year-old Princess Grace of Monaco dies tragically in a car crash.
B. U.S. Supreme Court Chief Justice Warren Burger gives up the gavel after nearly 20 years on the bench.
A. (1982) B. (1986)

HIT PARADE **Q:** What unlikely duo had a Top 10 hit in the '80s with "To All The Girls I've Loved Before"?
A: Julio Iglesias and Willie Nelson

DEAD OR ALIVE? River Phoenix (actor)
Alive. This Hollywood hottie OD'd on Sunset Boulevard in 1993.

BLAST FROM THE PAST

14

FACT OR PHOOEY? Prince (a.k.a. The Artist Formerly Known As) wrote the '80s dance anthem "I Feel For You," sung by Chaka Khan.
Fact.

HOT OR NOT? MTV
Hot. Debuting in 1981, the cable network changed the face of popular music. By the decade's end, MTV wasn't just playing superstars, it was making them.

RAPID RECALL Q: Which *Alice* waitress said, "Kiss my grits!"?
A: Flo

ORDER UP! **A.** Amy Tan receives literary accolades for her first novel, *The Joy Luck Club.*
B. Disney's man-made window on the world, the Epcot Center, opens for business.
B. (1982) A. (1989)

HIT PARADE Q: Both Van Halen and The Pointer Sisters had hits with what title in 1984?
A: "Jump"

DEAD OR ALIVE? Desmond Llewelyn (*James Bond*'s Q)
Alive. Q didn't call it quits till 1999.

BLAST FROM THE **PAST**

15

FACT OR PHOOEY? In the Dire Straits' song "Money For Nothing," Sting sings the "I want my MTV" line.
Fact.

HOT OR NOT? *Tiny Toon Adventures*
Not. Babs, Buster, and the rest of the new generation of Warner cartoons didn't start their wacky run until 1990.

RAPID RECALL **Q:** What country brought American teens Tetris?
A: Russia

ORDER UP! **A.** Halley's Comet makes a return visit to planet Earth.
B. *USA Today* goes to press, specializing in bite-sized news, color photos, and splashy graphics.
B. (1982) A. (1986)

HIT PARADE **Sing** a line from Prince's "When Doves Cry."

DEAD OR ALIVE? George Burns
Alive. Hollywood's favorite funnyman was still kicking till 1996.

BLAST FROM THE PAST

16

FACT OR PHOOEY? Wile E. Coyote never caught the Road Runner.
Phooey! He did so once, on May 21, 1980.

HOT OR NOT? *The Facts of Life*
Hot. You take the good, you take the bad, you take them both, and there you have this long running hit about Natalie, Blair, Jo, and Tootie.

RAPID RECALL **Q:** What is the name of the small New York company where the sitcom *Taxi* takes place?
A: The Sunshine Cab Company

ORDER UP! **A.** Mount St. Helens erupts in Washington, killing 22 people.
B. AZT wins FDA approval in the fight against AIDS.
A. (1980) B. (1987)

HIT PARADE **Sing** a line from the 1980s duet "Love Lift Us Up Where We Belong" **or** name one of the song's two singers.
A: Joe Cocker or Jennifer Warnes

DEAD OR ALIVE? Vladimir Nabokov (author)
Dead. The Russian author of *Lolita* closed the book in 1977.

BLAST FROM THE *PAST*

17

FACT OR PHOOEY? In the 1980s, McDonald's eliminated close to one million pounds of waste per year by making its drinking straws lighter.
Fact. 20 percent lighter, to be exact.

HOT OR NOT? *ER*
Not. NBC is no stranger to the hospital-centered drama, but it was *St. Elsewhere* — not *ER* — that had '80s viewers checking in every week.

RAPID RECALL **Q:** Not everybody knows that *Cheers'* bar manager, Sam "Mayday" Malone, used to pitch for what baseball team?
A: Boston Red Sox

ORDER UP! **A.** President Reagan calls the Soviet Union "an evil empire" and declares it "the focus of evil in the modern world."
B. U.S. President Reagan and Soviet leader Mikhail Gorbachev put their heads together in person for the first time.
A. (1983) B. (1985)

HIT PARADE **Q:** Name the Janet Jackson hit that contains the lyric: "With music by our side to break the color lines, let's work together to improve our way of life."
A: "Rhythm Nation"

DEAD OR ALIVE? Mario Puzo (author)
Alive. *The Godfather*'s father didn't die until 1999.

18

FACT OR PHOOEY? In 1980, the Yellow Pages mistakenly listed a Texas funeral home under Frozen Foods.
Fact.

HOT OR NOT? Friendship bracelets
Hot. Girls across the country carried bags of embroidery thread and notched pieces of cardboard, ready to weave a symbol of affection on a moment's notice.

RAPID RECALL Q: She-Ra, Princess of Power, is the cartoon sister of whom?
A: He-Man

ORDER UP! A. The vinyl record faces extinction with the introduction of noise-free compact discs.
B. People start popping Prozac for the first time in the U.S.
A. (1982) B. (1987)

HIT PARADE Q: On what did Starship build this city?
A: Rock and Roll (from "We Built This City")

DEAD OR ALIVE? DeForest Kelley (*Star Trek*'s Dr. Leonard McCoy)
Alive. "Bones" from the original *Star Trek* TV series lived until 1999.

BLAST FROM THE PAST

19

FACT OR PHOOEY? If a person had $1 million in 1980, it would be the same as having $1 billion in 2000.
Phooey! $1 million in 1980 equals more like $2 million in 2000. (Either way, it's a lot of money!)

HOT OR NOT? *Star Wars*
Hot. Between George Lucas and Ronald Reagan, *Star Wars* kept people talking well into the middle of the decade.

RAPID RECALL **Q:** What apparel company introduced the first stonewashed jeans to the United States?
A: Guess?

ORDER UP! **A.** Tom Wolfe satirizes status-grubbers in the best-selling fiction debut of the decade, *The Bonfire of the Vanities*.
B. *Time* magazine names Los Angeles Olympic organizing president Peter Ueberroth its Man of the Year.
B. (1984) A. (1987)

HIT PARADE **Sing** a line from the Michael Jackson song that featured a speaking part by Vincent Price.
A: "Thriller"

DEAD OR ALIVE? Lyndon B. Johnson (former U.S. president)
Dead. The Texas-born 36th President of the U.S. died in 1973.

BLAST FROM THE PAST

20

FACT OR PHOOEY? Before making it big in the '80s music scene, Flock of Seagulls front man Mike Score was a hairdresser.
Fact.

HOT OR NOT? Roller rinks
Hot. In the '80s it seemed that everybody was itching to lace up their Roller Derby skates and hit the floor.

RAPID RECALL **Q:** In the *A-Team*, what was group leader Colonel John Smith's nickname?
A: Hannibal

ORDER UP! **A.** Martin Scorsese's *Raging Bull* knocks out moviegoers.
B. Cycling poster-boy Greg LeMond pedals the way as the first American to win the Tour de France.
A. (1980) B. (1986)

HIT PARADE **Q:** What parody of Queen's 1981 hit "Another One Bites the Dust" did Weird Al release?
A: "Another One Rides The Bus"

DEAD OR ALIVE? Benny Hill (comedian)
Alive. Britain's bawdy comedian didn't bite the dust till 1992.

21

FACT OR PHOOEY? After cuts to the school lunch program in 1981, the U.S. Department of Agriculture declared that mustard counts as a vegetable.
Phooey! But they did declare ketchup a vegetable.

HOT OR NOT? *Home Alone*
Not. Director John Hughes ruled the '80s, but his biggest success, Macaulay Culkin's turn as a pint-sized home protector, came out in the '90s.

RAPID RECALL **Q:** On what night of the week did NBC's *The Cosby Show* air regularly on prime time TV?
A: Thursday

ORDER UP! **A.** *The Empire Strikes Back* at the box office.
B. 32-year-old Sally Ride becomes the first American woman in space.
A. (1980) B. (1983)

HIT PARADE **Sing** a line from "What I Like About You" or name the band that sang it.
A: The Romantics

DEAD OR ALIVE? Howard Hughes
Dead. The reclusive millionaire's spruce was goosed in 1976.

BLAST FROM THE PAST

22

FACT OR PHOOEY? The *Falcon Crest* family made their fortune breeding rare birds.
Phooey! They owned a vineyard.

HOT OR NOT? Bangle bracelets
Hot. Thin and easy to slide on, stacked bangles rose to the height of
'80s teen style.

RAPID RECALL Q: Which came first, *Fame* the movie or *Fame* the TV series?
A: *Fame* the movie

ORDER UP! **A.** Stephen Spielberg's *Raiders of the Lost Ark* rolls into theaters.
B. Presidential candidate Gary Hart gets caught monkeying
around with Donna Rice on board a boat named *Monkey
Business*.
A. (1981) B. (1987)

HIT PARADE Q: What 1980s Pretenders hit was subtitled "I'm Special"?
A: "Brass in Pocket"

DEAD OR ALIVE? Agatha Christie (mystery writer)
Dead. Christie wrote more than 80 books before her death in 1976.

BLAST FROM THE **PAST**

23

FACT OR PHOOEY? Before breaking into the big time, "Weird Al" Yankovic was an accordion teacher.
Fact.

HOT OR NOT? The V-chip
Not. Concerned parents would have to wait until the late '90s before they could program their TVs to automatically block content.

RAPID RECALL Q: Tenderheart, Love-A-Lot, and Funshine are all names of what group of cartoon characters?
A: The Care Bears

ORDER UP! **A.** Three American nuns are found dead in El Salvador.
B. A U.S. jury sends Oliver North to the slammer for his part in the Iran-Contra affair.
A. (1980) B. (1989)

HIT PARADE Q: Fill in the blanks in this 1983 hit: "Once upon a time I was falling in love but now I'm only falling apart, Nothing I can do, a _____ _____ ___ __ _____ "
A: Total eclipse of the heart (from "Total Eclipse of the Heart" by Bonnie Tyler)

DEAD OR ALIVE? Erma Bombeck (newspaper columnist/author)
Alive. The woman who wrote about household humor died in 1996.

BLAST FROM THE PAST

24

FACT OR PHOOEY? Charlie Sheen appears in *Ferris Bueller's Day Off.*
Fact.

HOT OR NOT? GI Joe®
Hot. The military man was back on the front lines in the '80s with a new line of posable action figures, a comic book, and a popular cartoon series.

RAPID RECALL **Q:** In the TV show *Fraggle Rock,* what is the name of the beings that live and rule beyond Fraggle Rock?
A: The Gorgs

ORDER UP! **A.** At age 59, Rock Hudson is the first star to publicly fall victim to AIDS.
B. Barney Clark becomes the first person to have an artificial heart transplant.
B. (1982) A. (1985)

HIT PARADE Q: Finish the line from this Pat Benatar hit: "You're a real tough cookie with a long history of . . ."
A: Breaking little hearts like the one in me (from "Hit Me With Your Best Shot")

DEAD OR ALIVE? Sam Giancana (mobster)
Dead. This Chicago mobster was "whacked" in 1975.

BLAST FROM **THE PAST**

25

FACT OR PHOOEY? Danielle Steel owned a dating service before she started writing romance novels.
Phooey! Steel got her start in the trenches, writing ad copy.

HOT OR NOT? The Carpenters
Not. The sibling songbirds' pop music reign came to an end in the early '80s when sister Karen succumbed to anorexia-related heart problems.

RAPID RECALL **Q:** According to a popular '80s sitcom, what does ALF stand for?
A: Alien life form

ORDER UP! **A.** Ronald Reagan is sworn in as the 40th U.S. president.
B. Kids go crazy for questionably cute Cabbage Patch dolls.
A. (1981) B. (1983)

HIT PARADE **Sing** a line from Toni Basil's one-hit '80s wonder, "Mickey."

DEAD OR ALIVE? Shari Lewis (Lamb Chop puppeteer)
Alive. Lamb Chop didn't lose its beloved right hand until 1998.

BLAST FROM THE PAST

26

FACT OR PHOOEY? Deee-lite's Lady Miss Kier received the official title of "Lady" after her mother married an English nobleman.
Phooey! Born Kieren Kirby in Youngstown, Ohio, Kier has no English family ties.

HOT OR NOT? "Read my lips: no new taxes"
Hot. George Bush's declaration became favored fodder for comedians in the late '80s.

RAPID RECALL **Q:** In the '80s sitcom *B. J. and the Bear,* what was B. J.'s occupation?
A: A trucker

ORDER UP! **A.** Terrorists hijack the *Achille Lauro,* an Italian cruise ship.
B. Moviegoers flock to *Field of Dreams.*
A. (1985) B. (1989)

HIT PARADE **Q:** What 1980s Kevin Bacon flik featured the hit "Let's Hear it For the Boy"?
A: *Footloose.*

DEAD OR ALIVE? Marlene Dietrich (actress)
Alive. The marvelous Ms. Dietrich didn't die till 1992.

BLAST FROM THE *PAST*

27

FACT OR PHOOEY? *The Nightmare on Elm Street*'s villain Freddy was named after a kid who used to bully Wes Craven as a child.
Fact.

HOT OR NOT? U.S. Olympic Champions
Hot. The '80s set new athletic standards, starting with the 1980 miracle hockey team and continuing with stars like Carl Lewis and Greg Louganis.

RAPID RECALL **Q:** Producer Glen Larson followed up his late 1970s *Battlestar Galactica* success with what other sci-fi series?
A: *Buck Rogers in the 25th Century*

ORDER UP! **A.** *Fatal Attraction* frightens would-be adulterers into fidelity.
B. "The Wall," designed by 22-year-old Yale University architecture student Mia Lin, is dedicated on Veterans' Day in Washington, D.C.
B. (1982) A. (1987)

HIT PARADE **Q:** Philip Bailey teamed with what more famous Phil for the hit "Easy Lover"?
A: Phil Collins

DEAD OR ALIVE? Jacques Cousteau (explorer)
Alive. The famous ocean explorer died in 1997.

28

FACT OR PHOOEY? Dolly Parton met her husband Carl Dean at a laundromat.
A: Fact. It was a Wishy-Washy Laundromat in Nashville, Tennessee.

HOT OR NOT? *Choose Your Own Adventures*
Hot. Kids went mad for these choice-filled fantasies in the '80s. Each book contained as many as 40 different endings.

RAPID RECALL **Q:** In what city does the sitcom *Full House* take place?
A: San Francisco

ORDER UP! **A.** James L. Brooks contributes to tissue sales and takes home the big prize at the Oscars® for *Terms of Endearment*.
B. Canadian runner Ben Johnson tests positive for steroids and is stripped of his Olympic gold.
A. (1983) B. (1988)

HIT PARADE **Q:** Sing a line from "Summer of '69" or name the singer.
A: Bryan Adams

DEAD OR ALIVE? Aristotle Onassis
Dead. Jackie O's Greek beau died in 1975.

BLAST FROM THE PAST

29

FACT OR PHOOEY? Country star Kenny Rogers starred as gambler Brady Hawkes in all five episodes of *The Gambler* mini-series.
Fact.

HOT OR NOT? Shaun Cassidy
Not. Brother of David (a.k.a. Keith Partridge), Shaun was a bona fide '70s pop star and pin-up. By the '80s, he'd dropped off the teenybopper radar.

RAPID RECALL **Q:** What 1980s drama starred the Six Million Dollar Man?
A: *The Fall Guy* starred Lee Majors

ORDER UP! **A.** President Reagan "dismisses" all striking air-traffic controllers who refused his return-to-work order.
B. Insider trading scandals shake Wall Street's white-collar world.
A. (1981) B. (1986)

HIT PARADE **Q:** In 1986 OMD had a hit with "If You Leave." What do the letters OMD stand for?
A: Orchestral Manoeuvres In the Dark

DEAD OR ALIVE? Elvis Presley (musician)
Dead. The King of Rock-n-Roll died in 1977, baby.

BLAST FROM THE *PAST*

30

FACT OR PHOOEY? In the 1982 Steven Spielberg blockbuster, E.T. dresses up as Yoda for Halloween.
Phooey! E.T. dresses up as a ghost.

HOT OR NOT? Body piercing
Not. Boys with earrings were no longer a shock in the '80s, but nose and eyebrow rings didn't hit the mainstream till well into the next decade.

RAPID RECALL **Q:** What profession did the character Maddie Hayes on *Moonlighting* hold before becoming a private detective?
A: Fashion model

ORDER UP! **A.** A winning (and some say whiny) new drama, *thirtysomething*, debuts on ABC.
B. A massive earthquake strikes San Francisco.
A. (1987) B. (1989)

HIT PARADE **Q:** Finish the phrase from this early Madonna hit that gave her one of her many nicknames: "Some boys kiss me, some boys hug me, _____"
A: I think they're ok (from "Material Girl")

DEAD OR ALIVE? Leonard Bernstein (composer)
Alive. The *West Side Story* composer died in 1990.

BLAST FROM THE PAST

31

FACT OR PHOOEY? From 1980 to 1988, a new Concorde was produced every two years.
Phooey! Only sixteen were ever made. The last one was completed in 1980.

HOT OR NOT? Hair tails
Hot. Bored with a bowl cut? Keep a small section of hair at the nape of your neck and grow a tail. Left loose or braided, tails were hot for him (and her) in the '80s.

RAPID RECALL **Q:** What *Happy Days* actor created the popular '80s drama *MacGyver*?
A: Henry Winkler

ORDER UP! **A.** Andrew Lloyd Weber's *The Phantom of the Opera* takes the Tony for best musical.
B. Dustin Hoffman plays Michael Dorsey playing Dorothy Michaels in Sydney Pollack's *Tootsie*.
B. (1982) A. (1988)

HIT PARADE **Sing** a line from Bruce Springsteen's "Born in the USA."

DEAD OR ALIVE? Wolfman Jack (D.J.)
Alive. The famed D.J. who appeared as himself in *American Graffiti* died in 1995.

32

FACT OR PHOOEY? A new movie rating, PG-15, was introduced in 1984.
Phooey! PG-13 was the new rating in '84.

HOT OR NOT? HyperColor shirts
Hot. These hi-tech tees enjoyed hype in the '80s. But like the handprints left on them, HyperColor eventually faded out of fashion.

RAPID RECALL **Q:** Operation Evening Light (or Eagle Claw) was the name given to the U.S. attempt to rescue American hostages held by what country?
A: Iran

ORDER UP! **A.** Kids demand quarters as Pac-Man mania sweeps the country.
B. A French court sentences 73-year-old Gestapo wartime chief Klaus Barbie to life in prison for WWII war crimes.
A. (1981) B. (1987)

HIT PARADE **Sing** a line from Joan Jett and the Blackhearts' "I Love Rock and Roll."

DEAD OR ALIVE? Mao Tse-tung (a.k.a. Mao Zedong)
Dead. The Chinese leader died in 1976.

BLAST FROM THE PAST

33

FACT OR PHOOEY? Hormel had sold over three billion cans of Spam® throughout the world by the start of the '80s.
Fact.

HOT OR NOT? Magic Eye® images
Not. These 3-D images hidden in computer-generated patterns didn't appear until the '90s.

RAPID RECALL **Q:** What actress played Tony Danza's daughter on *Who's The Boss*?
A: Alyssa Milano

ORDER UP! **A.** Tens of thousands of Chinese students demonstrate for democracy in Beijing's Tiananmen Square.
B. The U.S. Supreme Court says taping television shows at home on your VCR is not a crime.
B. (1984) A. (1989)

HIT PARADE **Q:** What triply-titled Genesis song contained the lyric "Try to shake it loose, cut it free, let it go, get it away from me"?
A: "Tonight, Tonight, Tonight"

DEAD OR ALIVE? Norman Rockwell (artist)
Dead. The illustrator, best known for his touching and humorous portraits of American life, died in 1978.

BLAST FROM THE PAST

34

FACT OR PHOOEY? The sitcom *Kate & Allie* caused controversy for featuring two gay single mothers.
Phooey! Kate and Allie were criticized because they were divorcees.

HOT OR NOT? The Brat Pack
Hot. This troupe of young actors ruled Hollywood in the '80s. Now most of their names just leave people wondering, "Where are they now?"

RAPID RECALL **Q:** Which New Kid on the Block grew up to be *Boogie Night*'s Dirk Digler?
A: Donnie Wahlberg

ORDER UP! **A.** Oliver North takes the Fifth in the Iran-Contra investigation.
B. Christopher Cross sails away with multiple Grammys, winning for best album, song, record, and new artist of the year.
B. (1980) A. (1987)

HIT PARADE **Q:** What right did The Beastie Boys want you to fight for in 1987?
A: Your right to party (from "(You Gotta) Fight for Your Right (to Party)")

DEAD OR ALIVE? John Wayne
Dead. The Duke died of lung cancer in 1979.

BLAST FROM THE *PAST*

35

FACT OR PHOOEY? *Murder, She Wrote* was the longest-running and most watched detective series in American TV history.
Fact.

HOT OR NOT? He-Man
Hot. He might have been only 6 inches tall and made out of plastic, but He-Man and his cohorts had the power to keep kids interested during the '80s.

RAPID RECALL **Q:** In what planet Earth city did Mork and Mindy share an apartment?
A: Boulder, Colorado

ORDER UP! **A.** Don Johnson and Philip Michael Thomas make a pastel fashion statement on *Miami Vice*.
B. Toni Morrison picks up the Pulitzer for *Beloved*.
A. (1981) B. (1988)

HIT PARADE **Q:** Fill in the blanks from this 1987 hit from a rocking Irish import: "I have climbed the highest mountains, I have run through the fields, only to __ _____ ___."
A: Be with you (From U2's "I Still Haven't Found What I'm Looking For")

DEAD OR ALIVE? Eva Gabor
Alive. The *Green Acres* actress and sister of Zsa-Zsa died in 1995.

BLAST FROM THE PAST

36

FACT OR PHOOEY? Janet Jackson sang on the "We Are the World" single.
Phooey! Janet didn't have a part in the hit song, although her sister LaToya did.

HOT OR NOT? "Hair" rock bands
Hot. '80s hair defied the laws of gravity (and good taste) with groups like Poison and Bon Jovi.

RAPID RECALL **Q:** What movie had people across the country arguing over whether men and women can "just be friends"?
A: *When Harry Met Sally*

ORDER UP! **A.** New York subway "vigilante" Bernhard Goetz shoots four African American teenagers on a train in Manhattan.
B. American financier and junk bond junkie Michael Milken is nailed for insider trading.
A. (1984) B. (1988)

HIT PARADE **Sing** a line (other than the chorus) from R.E.M's "End of the World."

DEAD OR ALIVE? Betty Grable
Dead. WWII's most famous pin-up girl died in 1973.

BLAST FROM **THE PAST**

37

FACT OR PHOOEY? Lead actor Ralph Macchio was 28 years old when *The Karate Kid III* was released in 1989.
Fact. A 28-year-old kid?

HOT OR NOT? Colorforms®
Hot. The vinyl play pieces that stick like magic had already been around for thirty years in the '80s, but playsets based on popular cartoons kept kids begging for them in the age of video games.

RAPID RECALL **Q:** What is the title of the first Rambo movie?
A: *First Blood*

ORDER UP! **A.** British scientists discover a BIG hole in the Earth's ozone layer over Antarctica.
B. Tom Hanks stars as a kid stuck in a grown-up's body in *Big*.
A. (1985) B. (1988)

HIT PARADE **Q:** What Def Leppard song asked the question, "Demolition woman, can I be your man?"
A: "Pour Some Sugar on Me"

DEAD OR ALIVE? Keith Haring (contemporary artist)
Alive. The '80s "It" artist died from an AIDS-related illness in 1990.

BLAST FROM THE PAST

38

FACT OR PHOOEY? The Statue of Liberty turned 200 in 1986.
Phooey! Lady Liberty celebrated her 100th in 1986.

HOT OR NOT? Nolan Ryan
Hot. Baseball's "iron man" pitcher proved he was anything but over the hill in the '80s. In 1989, he threw his 5,000th career strikeout.

RAPID RECALL Q: What English movie beat out the competition to win 1982's Best Picture award at the Oscars®?
A: *Chariots of Fire*

ORDER UP! **A.** Chicago Bears running back Walter Payton breaks Jim Brown's lifetime rushing record of 12,213 yards.
B. CDs outsell vinyl records for the first time.
A. (1984) B. (1988)

HIT PARADE Q: What mother-daughter duo had a hit with "Rocking with the Rhythm of the Rain"?
A: The Judds

DEAD OR ALIVE? Margaux Hemingway (actress)
Alive. Hemingway didn't commit suicide until July 2, 1996, the anniversary of the suicide of her famous grandfather.

BLAST *FROM* **THE** *PAST*

39

FACT OR PHOOEY? *Growing Pains'* Tracey Gold and *Benson*'s Missy Gold are twins.
Phooey! The Gold girls are sisters, but Tracey is just a little more than a year older than Missy.

HOT OR NOT? Magic: The Gathering
Not. Fantasy-based games were big in the '80s, but it was Dungeons and Dragons that ruled the imagination. Magic: The Gathering didn't appear until 1994.

RAPID RECALL **Ω:** What actor's scenes ended up on the cutting room floor during editing of 1983's box office hit *The Big Chill*?
A: Kevin Costner

ORDER UP! **A.** The *Exxon Valdez* strikes a reef in Alaska, spilling 11 million gallons of oil into the Prince William Sound and devastating the eco-system.
B. Madonna hits the road like a virgin, on tour for the very first time.
B. (1985) A. (1989)

HIT PARADE **Sing** a line from Guns 'n' Roses "Sweet Child of Mine."

DEAD OR ALIVE? Morris the Cat (9Lives® cat)
Dead. TV's original Morris lived his last life in 1978.

BLAST FROM THE PAST

40

FACT OR PHOOEY? The United Colors of Benetton is an English company.
Finto! Luciano Benetton founded the company in Italy.

HOT OR NOT? M. C. Hammer
Not. Hammer's baggy pants and distinctive sound couldn't be touched by anyone, but he didn't hit the big time till 1990.

RAPID RECALL **Q:** What U.S. military branch does Richard Gere's character in *An Officer and a Gentleman* belong to?
A: The Navy

ORDER UP! **A.** Oprah debuts on daytime and begins her rise to media-moguldom.
B. Alice Walker pockets a Pulitzer (and the National Book Award) for *The Color Purple*.
B. (1983) A. (1986)

HIT PARADE **Q:** What former New Edition member hit the top of the charts with "My Prerogative"?
A: Bobby Brown

DEAD OR ALIVE? Joan Crawford (actress)
Dead. Mommie Dearest died in 1977.

BLAST FROM **THE PAST**

41

FACT OR PHOOEY? Model Christie Brinkley was the face of Cover Girl cosmetics throughout the 1980s.
Fact.

HOT OR NOT? Nintendo
Hot. With the help of two portly Italian plumbers, August 1985 saw the birth of a new obsession: Nintendo.

RAPID RECALL **Q:** In *The Breakfast Club,* what is the one trick Claire can do that she demonstrates for the others?
A: Apply lipstick with no hands

ORDER UP! **A.** Several former White House officials reveal that first lady Nancy Reagan uses astrology to help her husband make decisions.
B. Ted Turner makes headlines with the launch of CNN, the first all-news network.
B. (1980) A. (1988)

HIT PARADE **Q:** What popular 1980s soundtrack featured Eric Carmen's "Hungry Eyes"?
A: *Dirty Dancing*

DEAD OR ALIVE? Gianni Versace (fashion designer)
Alive. Versace was a leader of the fashion world up until his murder in 1997.

BLAST FROM THE PAST

42

FACT OR PHOOEY?   Roxette's hit "Dangerous" was first offered to and turned down by *Miami Vice*'s Don Johnson.
Fact.

HOT OR NOT?   Sonny and Cher
Not. The dynamic duo went their separate ways after their 1974 divorce.

RAPID RECALL   Q: Where could you buy a Big Gulp in the 1980s?
A: At a 7-Eleven store (You still can!)

ORDER UP!   **A.** Dozens of top-drawer musicians fill the bill at Live Aid concerts, hoping to "feed the world."
B. In a failed attempt to impress actress Jodie Foster, John Hinckley, Jr. shoots President Reagan and three others.
B. (1981) A. (1985)

HIT PARADE   Q: What band shares its name with a U.S. state and had a hit in the '80s with "Mountain Music"?
A: Alabama

DEAD OR ALIVE?   Bobby Darin (singer)
Dead. The "Mack the Knife" singer died in 1973.

BLAST FROM THE *PAST*

43

FACT OR PHOOEY? Cher won a Cannes Film Festival award for her role in the 1980s tearjerker *The Elephant Man*.
Phooey! Cher won the coveted Cannes award for her role in *Mask*.

HOT OR NOT? Benefit concerts
Hot. Band Aid, Live Aid, Farm Aid, USA for Africa—musicians of the '80s turned charity into high profile rock and roll extravaganzas.

RAPID RECALL **Q:** What burger chain asked "Where's the Beef?" in a popular 1980s ad campaign?
A: Wendy's

ORDER UP! **A.** Benazir Bhutto is elected prime minister of Pakistan, the first woman to hold this office in any modern Islamic state.
B. John McEnroe wins Wimbledon for the third year in a row.
B. (1981) A. (1988)

HIT PARADE **Q:** Fill in the blanks from this Bangles hit: "Six o'clock already, I was just in the middle of a dream. I was kissin' _____ by a crystal blue _____ _____."
A: Valentino, Italian stream (from "Manic Monday")

DEAD OR ALIVE? Freddie Prinze (actor)
Dead. The co-star of TV's *Chico and the Man* died at age 22 in 1977.

BLAST FROM THE PAST

44

FACT OR PHOOEY? Heather O'Rourke, child star of all three *Poltergeist* movies, died at the age of 12 from septic shock.
Fact.

HOT OR NOT? *The Six Million Dollar Man*
Not. Lee Majors as the man rebuilt better, stronger and faster was a phenomenon in the '70s, but by the '80s the power was gone.

RAPID RECALL **Q:** What popular Christian television program, the first of its kind, did Tammy Faye and Jim Bakker help create?
A: *The 700 Club*

ORDER UP! **A.** Crooner Karen Carpenter dies of complications from anorexia nervosa at age 32.
B. In an attempt to drive General Manuel Noriega from his hideout, the U.S. military blasts rock music at the Panamanian bad boy 24/7.
A. (1983) B. (1989)

HIT PARADE **Sing** a line from Robert Palmer's "Addicted to Love."

DEAD OR ALIVE? Jim Henson (Muppets creator)
Alive. The man who gave life to Miss Piggy and Kermit the Frog died in May of 1990 from a severe strep infection.

45

FACT OR PHOOEY?   In 1980, Jean Marie Butler became the first woman to graduate from any U.S. service academy.
Fact. She graduated from the U.S. Coast Guard Academy.

HOT OR NOT?   Chia Pets
Hot. You didn't need a green thumb to grow to love these low maintenance companions, first popularized in the '80s.

RAPID RECALL   **Q:** Bruce Willis and Mel Gibson began what two strings of action movies in the late 1980s?
A: *Die Hard* and *Lethal Weapon*

ORDER UP!   **A.** Iran's Ayatollah Khomeini puts a bounty on the head of *The Satanic Verses* author, Salman Rushdie.
B. Mark David Chapman shoots and kills Beatle John Lennon on a New York sidewalk.
B. (1980) A. (1989)

HIT PARADE   **Q:** "Shot through the heart, and you're to blame," Bon Jovi says, "You give ____ _ ___ ____."
A: Love a bad name (from "You Give Love A Bad Name")

DEAD OR ALIVE?   J. Edgar Hoover (FBI director)
Dead. The FBI's very first director died in 1972.

BLAST FROM THE PAST

46

FACT OR PHOOEY? Tom Cruise stars as disabled Vietnam vet turned antiwar activist Ron Kovick in 1989's *Born on the Fourth of July*.
Fact.

HOT OR NOT? Studio 54
Not. The glory days of this Eden of excess came to an end in 1979 when its owners were arrested for tax evasion.

RAPID RECALL **Q:** What 1986 game gave American kids their first case of Nintendo fever and sold more than one million copies?
A: *The Legend of Zelda*

ORDER UP! **A.** Teary-eyed televangelist Jimmy Swaggart admits having "known" a prostitute (or two).
B. Season ticket holders and die-hard fans cry foul during a 50-day major league baseball strike.
B. (1981) A. (1988)

HIT PARADE **Sing** a line from teen queen Debbie Gibson's "Shake Your Love."

DEAD OR ALIVE? Gene Kelly (actor)
Alive. The *Singing in the Rain* star died in 1996.

BLAST FROM **THE PAST**

47

FACT OR PHOOEY? 1989's *Do the Right Thing* was Spike Lee's directorial debut.
Phooey! Lee made several movies before *Do the Right Thing,* including *She's Gotta Have It* and *School Daze.*

HOT OR NOT? Sandra Day O'Connor
Hot. She is woman, hear her rule. In 1981 Sandra Day O'Connor became the first female Supreme Court Justice.

RAPID RECALL **Q:** 1980s hit makers Duran Duran sang the theme song to what killer James Bond movie?
A: *A View To a Kill*

ORDER UP! **A.** Alan Greenspan replaces Paul Volcker as Federal Reserve Chairman.
B. In a mysterious move, the U.S. invades Grenada.
B. (1983) A. (1987)

HIT PARADE **Q:** What country crooner won a Grammy in 1980 for "On the Road Again"?
A: Willie Nelson

DEAD OR ALIVE? Michael Hutchence (of INXS)
Alive. This famous front man rocked on until his mysterious death in 1997.

BLAST FROM THE PAST

48

FACT OR PHOOEY? Between 1980 and 1989, the U.S. federal debt went from a whopping $909.1 billion to a whopping $2868.0 billion.
Fact.

HOT OR NOT? Televangelists
Hot. TV "parishes" popped up—and fell from grace—in the '80s.

RAPID RECALL **Q:** What company did a 20-year-old Canadian hockey player start in 1980 that had roller-skate makers running scared?
A: Rollerblade, Inc.

ORDER UP! **A.** The space shuttle *Challenger* explodes on national TV, killing all seven crewmembers in the tragedy.
B. San Diego zookeepers become the proud parents of four California condors, the first to be hatched in captivity.
B. (1983) A. (1986)

HIT PARADE **Q:** What British ska band hit the American Top 10 in 1983 with "Our House"?
A: Madness

DEAD OR ALIVE? Groucho Marx
Dead. The head of the classic comic quartet died in 1977.

BLAST FROM THE PAST

49

FACT OR PHOOEY?   Noah Wylie played Goose in the 1986 movie *Top Gun*.
Phooey! Anthony Edwards, Wylie's *ER* co-star, played Goose.

HOT OR NOT?   "Just Say No"
Hot. Nancy Reagan's drug prevention catch phrase caught fire in the early '80s, and became the butt of countless jokes.

RAPID RECALL   **Q:** What half of the 1980s hit-making duo Wham! went on to solo pop stardom?
A: George Michael

ORDER UP!   **A.** Tampons are deemed dubious after Toxic Shock Syndrome strikes a reported 400 women.
B. The Dow's one-day drop of 508 points becomes know as "Black Monday."
A. (1980) B. (1987)

HIT PARADE   **Q:** What group cried, "Shout, shout/Let it all out . . ." in a 1985 release?
A: Tears for Fears (from "Shout" on *Songs From the Big Chair*)

DEAD OR ALIVE?   Dean Martin (actor)
Alive. The legendary Rat Packer didn't pack it in until 1995.

BLAST FROM THE PAST

50

FACT OR PHOOEY? The "time machine" in *Back to the Future* is a Corvette.
Phooey! It's a DeLorean.

HOT OR NOT? Pop Rocks
Hot. No one *really* died from mixing Pop Rocks and soda, but kids loved the legend almost as much as the candy.

RAPID RECALL Q: What hour-long TV show starred Stephanie Powers and Robert Wagner as married detectives?
A: *Hart to Hart*

ORDER UP! **A.** At just under five feet tall, 16-year-old gymnast Mary Lou Retton is the pint-sized darling of the Los Angeles Olympic games.
B. In a remarkable upset, the U.S. hockey team topples the Russians at the Lake Placid Winter Olympics.
B. (1980) A. (1984)

HIT PARADE Q: What familial country duo bridged the generation gap with the release of "Tear in My Beer" in 1989?
A: Hank Williams and Hank Williams, Jr.

DEAD OR ALIVE? Charles Atlas (body builder)
Dead. The famous muscle man was born in 1892 and died in 1972.

BLAST FROM THE **PAST**

51

FACT OR PHOOEY? *Hill Street Blues* takes place in Philadelphia, Pennsylvania.
Phooey! The setting is never mentioned on the show, but exterior shots were filmed in Chicago, Illinois.

HOT OR NOT? New Coke
Not. Introduced in 1985, Coke's new formula fizzled. In response to public outcry, the company quickly went back to the good old-fashioned version.

RAPID RECALL **Q:** What supermodel made moles fashionable?
A: Cindy Crawford

ORDER UP! **A.** Pan-Am Flight 103 explodes over Lockerbie, Scotland, killing all 259 aboard and 11 people on the ground.
B. Soda-lovers start saving calories by guzzling diet colas sweetened with NutraSweet®. Yum!
B. (1983) A. (1988)

HIT PARADE **Sing/say** a line from The Fresh Prince (Will Smith)'s first hit song ("Parents Just Don't Understand").

DEAD OR ALIVE? Maurice Chevalier (actor/singer)
Dead. The French singer and *Gigi* actor died in 1972.

BLAST FROM THE PAST

52

FACT OR PHOOEY? Swatch® prototypes were first test marketed in the U.S.A. in 1982.
Fact. By 1983, Swatches were available worldwide.

HOT OR NOT? The Walkman®
Hot. These revolutionary portable players were an '80s must-have.

RAPID RECALL Q: Susan Dey, also known as *The Partridge Family's* Laurie, went on to practice law on what TV program?
A: *L.A. Law*

ORDER UP! **A.** Twenty-one-year-old American speed skater Eric Heiden picks up a record-breaking five individual gold medals at the Lake Placid winter Olympics.
B. Famed architect I. M. Pei designs a new entrance for Paris' Louvre museum, a much-debated glass pyramid.
A. (1980) B. (1989)

HIT PARADE Q: According to Ray Parker Jr.'s 1984 hit song, "If there's something strange in your neighborhood,/ Who you gonna call?"
A: Ghostbusters!

DEAD OR ALIVE? Colleen Dewhurst (actress)
Alive. This *Anne of Green Gables* star died in 1991.

53

FACT OR PHOOEY? Barbara Billingsly (of *Leave It To Beaver* fame) was the voice of Animal on *The Muppet Babies* cartoon.
Phooey! Billingsly was the soothing voice of Nanny.

HOT OR NOT? *The Cosby Show*
Hot. Long before Must-See TV, the Huxtable clan kept folks tuned to NBC.

RAPID RECALL **Q:** What money-minded New York street provides the title of the 1987 movie starring Michael Douglas and Charlie Sheen?
A: Wall Street

ORDER UP! **A.** Under pressure from conservatives, a Washington D.C. art gallery cancels its controversial Robert Mapplethorpe exhibit.
B. Scientists develop the first genetically engineered plant approved for sale: a tomato, affectionately dubbed the Flavr Savr.
B. (1982) A. (1989)

HIT PARADE **Q:** Murry Head topped the charts with a song about one night in what Southeast Asian city?
A: Bangkok

DEAD OR ALIVE? Ronnie van Zant (musician)
Dead. This Lynyrd Skynyrd member died in a 1977 plane crash.

BLAST FROM THE PAST

54

FACT OR PHOOEY? Pee-Wee Herman's bow tie was baby blue.
Phooey! Pee-Wee's signature bow tie was red.

HOT OR NOT? **Hot or Not.** Strawberry Shortcake
Hot. Ms. Shortcake and her fruit-scented friends were enough to freshen any girl's toy box or dollhouse in the '80s.

RAPID RECALL **Q:** What comedian carved a niche for himself as the Church Lady on *Saturday Night Live*?
A: Dana Carvey

ORDER UP! **A.** The U.S. loses the America's Cup to the Aussies, the first defeat for the U.S. since 1851.
B. A major earthquake rocks Mexico, killing 10,000 people.
A. (1983) B. (1985)

HIT PARADE **Q:** Who was Prince's love interest in *Purple Rain*?
A: Apollonia

DEAD OR ALIVE? Fred MacMurray (actor)
Alive. The star of Disney's *The Shaggy Dog* and *The Absent-Minded Professor* died in 1991.

55

FACT OR PHOOEY?   1986's *Transformers: The Movie* featured Orson Welles as the evil Unicron.
Fact. Welles' *Transformers* role was one of his final performances.

HOT OR NOT?   *Are You Afraid of the Dark?*
Not. Nickelodeon's kid friendly twist on *Tales from the Crypt* and *The Twilight Zone* didn't hit the air until1992.

RAPID RECALL   **Q:** After his *WKRP in Cincinnati* stint, Howard Hesseman starred as Mr. Moore, a teacher on what ABC sitcom?
A: *Head of the Class*

ORDER UP!   **A.** Britain and Argentina go to war over the Falkland Islands.
B. Boston Red Sox pitcher Roger Clemens strikes out a record 20 batters in a row.
A. (1982) B. (1986)

HIT PARADE   **Sing** a line from the 1987 country hit "Forever and Ever, Amen" or name the singer.
A: Randy Travis

DEAD OR ALIVE?   Audrey Hepburn (actress)
Alive. *Breakfast at Tiffany's* Holly Golightly graced the world with her presence until her death in1993.

BLAST FROM **THE PAST**

56

FACT OR PHOOEY? The makers of Underoos launched Joe Boxer, the fun-to-wear underwear for adults in 1984.
Phooey! Former graphic designer Nicholas Graham started Joe Boxer.

HOT OR NOT? Skinny ties
Hot. The buttoned down look got an upgrade in the '80s when skinny ties were favored by groups like The Cars.

RAPID RECALL **Q:** Name three of the four "Golden Girls."
A: Dorothy (Beatrice Arthur), Rose (Betty White), Blanche (Rue McClanahan), and Sophia (Estelle Getty)

ORDER UP! **B.** In protest of the 1979 Soviet invasion of Afghanistan, the U.S. Olympic committee votes to boycott the Moscow Summer Games. **A.** After 20 years at the helm, President Ferdinand Marcos, his wife Imelda, and lots of her shoes flee the Philippines.
B. (1980) A. (1986)

HIT PARADE **Sing** a line from the Bobby McFerrin hit that became a cultural catch phrase.
A: "Don't Worry, Be Happy"

DEAD OR ALIVE? Mickey Mantle (baseball player)
Alive. This Baseball Hall of Famer took his final slide into home in 1995.

BLAST FROM THE PAST

57

FACT OR PHOOEY? Before she hit the big time, Jennifer Lopez was the choreographer for the Fly Girls, featured on *In Living Color*.
Phooey! J-Lo danced with the Fly Girls, but it was Rosie Perez who did the choreography.

HOT OR NOT? Ray Bans®
Hot. Just ask Tom Cruise and he'll tell you these shades were the finishing touch to any outfit, even if the pants were missing.

RAPID RECALL Q: What is the name given to the comedic puppet featured on the dance-themed television show *Solid Gold*?
A: Madame

ORDER UP! **B.** Seven people die after taking tampered Tylenol in Chicago, Illinois.
A. 20-year-old "Iron" Mike Tyson KOs Trevor Berbick, and makes heavyweight history as the youngest champ.
B. (1982) A. (1986)

HIT PARADE Q: In what 1988 song did Michael Jackson say, "If you wanna make the world a better place, take a look in the mirror and make a change"?
A: "Man in the Mirror"

DEAD OR ALIVE? Golda Meir (Israel Prime Minister)
Dead. Israel's fourth Prime Minister died in 1978.

1990s

BLAST FROM THE PAST

1

FACT OR PHOOEY?   The Powerpuff girls all have names starting with the letter P.
Phooey! The Powerpuff Girls all have names starting with B: Blossom, Buttercup, and Bubbles.

HOT OR NOT?   Play Station 2
Not. The hype started in the late '90s, but Sony's system was barely on the market in time for gamers to play before the new millennium.

RAPID RECALL   **Q:** Budweiser introduced a new ad campaign in a 1995 Super Bowl commercial featuring what animal?
A: Bullfrog

ORDER UP!   **A.** European countries agree on a single currency, called the Euro.
B. U.S. agents arrest General Manual Noriega of Panama on charges of drug dealing.
B. (1990) A. (1998)

HIT PARADE   **Sing** a line from Nirvana's breakthrough hit "Smells like Teen Spirit."

DEAD OR ALIVE?   Ray Kroc (McDonald's founder)
Dead. Fast food's big cheese bit the dust in 1984.

BLAST FROM THE PAST

2

FACT OR PHOOEY? M&M's introduced red to the candy bag's classic colors of yellow, orange, brown, and green in 1995.
Phooey! Blue was chosen as the new color for M&M's in 1995. Red was one of the original colors and is still part of the mix.

HOT OR NOT? Big Band Swing
Hot. The music of the '40s came back in full swing with a little help from Gap ads and films like *Swingers*.

RAPID RECALL **Q:** What 1992 vampire spoof movie launched a successful TV series starring Sarah Michelle Gellar?
A: *Buffy the Vampire Slayer*

ORDER UP! **A.** F.B.I. arrests Ted Kaczynski as a suspect in the "Unabomber" case.
B. The HBO series *The Sopranos* cleans up at the Emmys.
A. (1996) B. (1999)

HIT PARADE **Q:** Name two of the three brothers that took "MMMBop" to number one in 1997.
A: Isaac, Taylor, or Zac Hanson

DEAD OR ALIVE? Dale Evans
Alive. The "Queen of the West" and wife of Roy Rogers died in 2001.

BLAST FROM THE *PAST*

3

FACT OR PHOOEY? All of the clocks in the movie *Pulp Fiction* are stuck on 4:20.
Fact.

HOT OR NOT? Halley's Comet
Not. This once-in-a-lifetime comet made its most recent appearance in 1986.

RAPID RECALL Q: Jason, Zack, Trini, Kimberly, and Billy are all characters' names on what popular kids' television series?
A: *Mighty Morphin' Power Rangers*

ORDER UP! **A.** President George Bush and Russian president Boris Yeltsin proclaim a formal end to the Cold War.
B. Princess Di and her boyfriend Dodi Fayed die in a Paris car crash.
A. (1992) B. (1997)

HIT PARADE **Put on your dancing shoes** and do the Macarena **or** name the group who took it to the Top 10.
A: Los Del Rio

DEAD OR ALIVE? Dian Fossey (scientist)
Dead. The *Gorillas in the Mist* guru was found murdered in the African jungle in 1985.

BLAST FROM THE PAST

FACT OR PHOOEY? TV spokeswoman Wendy Kaufman was working the drive-through at McDonald's when Snapple® producers "discovered" her.
A. Phooey! Wendy was working at Snapple doing what audiences saw her doing on TV (answering consumer letters) when she got the job.

HOT OR NOT? *That 70s Show*
Hot. With a cast that included a former Charlie's Angel, Fox had an instant hit with the 1998 debut of this nostalgia trip.

RAPID RECALL Ω: What is the first name of the bike messenger booted out by his roommates on MTV's *Real World: San Francisco*?
A: Puck

ORDER UP! **A.** O. J. Simpson is arrested in connection with the killings of his wife, Nicole Brown Simpson, and her friend Ronald Goldman.
B. President Clinton denies allegations of an affair with White House intern Monica Lewinsky.
A. (1994) B. (1998)

HIT PARADE **Sing** a line from the over-played Whitney Houston song that was the theme from *The Bodyguard*.
A: "I Will Always Love You"

DEAD OR ALIVE? Jim Backus (*Gilligan's Island*'s Thurston Howell III)
Dead. Lovie's love and the voice of Mr. Magoo died in 1989.

5

FACT OR PHOOEY? Sharon Stone starred in 1991's *Terminator 2: Judgment Day* with Arnold Schwarzenegger.
Phooey! Stone starred in *Total Recall,* released in 1990. Linda Hamilton was the female lead in *T2.*

HOT OR NOT? Collectible lunch boxes
Not. With the 1985 national ban on metal lunch boxes, sacks were back by the '90s.

RAPID RECALL **Q:** Who played Wednesday in *The Addams Family* film, released in 1991?
A: Christina Ricci

ORDER UP! **A.** John F. Kennedy, Jr., his wife, and her sister are lost at sea when their private plane goes down near Massachusetts' Martha's Vineyard.
B. Robin Williams stars as a cross-dressing nanny in *Mrs. Doubtfire.*
B. (1993) A. (1999)

HIT PARADE **Q:** What band sang the following lyrics: "King Jeremy the wicked, oh, ruled his world/ Jeremy spoke in class today" in their 1995 smash single?
A: Pearl Jam ("Jeremy")

DEAD OR ALIVE? Morton Downey, Jr. (TV talk show host)
Alive. '80s trash TV's reigning king lived until 2001.

BLAST FROM THE PAST

6

FACT OR PHOOEY?   Director Francis Ford Coppola's first choice for Mary in *The Godfather Part III* was Winona Ryder, not his daughter Sofia.
Fact.

HOT OR NOT?   DJ Jazzy Jeff and The Fresh Prince
Not. "Parents Just Don't Understand" was a huge hit for the duo in 1988, but by the '90s the Prince (Will Smith) had moved on to bigger things.

RAPID RECALL   **Q:** What boy band asked audiences to "quit playing games" with their hearts on their 1996 self-titled album?
A: The Backstreet Boys

ORDER UP!   **A.** An outbreak of "mad cow" disease alarms Britain.
B. An estimated 76 million viewers watch the last episode of *Seinfeld.*
A. (1996) B. (1998)

HIT PARADE   **Q:** In 1991, what crooner became the first country artist to break the 10 million-seller mark?
A: Garth Brooks (with *No Fences*)

DEAD OR ALIVE?   Peter Lawford (actor)
Dead. The Rat Pack member and Kennedy in-law died in 1984.

BLAST FROM THE PAST

7

FACT OR PHOOEY? Whoopi Goldberg won an Academy Award® for her role as Oda Mae Brown in *Ghost*.
Fact. Goldberg's win made her the second African American woman in history to take home an Oscar®.

HOT OR NOT? *Quantum Leap*
Hot. The time and body jumping adventures of Dr. Sam Beckett kept viewers glued to their seats until the last episode in 1993.

RAPID RECALL **Q:** What was the cost to mail a letter in 1992?
A: 29 cents

ORDER UP! **A.** A nerve gas attack in a Tokyo subway kills eight and injures thousands.
B. TV viewers tune in to the Judge Clarence Thomas–Anita Hill sexual harassment hearings.
B. (1991) A. (1995)

HIT PARADE **Q:** Teen R&B princesses Monica and Brandy collaborated on what 1998 hit?
A: "The Boy is Mine"

DEAD OR ALIVE? William Hewlett (Hewlett-Packard co-founder)
Alive. This industry king didn't cash it in till 2001.

BLAST FROM THE PAST

8

FACT OR PHOOEY? Martha Stewart launched her own line of bed and bath products at Target in 1997.
Phooey! The home and garden mogul launched her line at Kmart.

HOT OR NOT? Grunge
Hot. The release of Nirvana's *Nevermind* album in 1991 ushered in a gritty new sound and look on the American music scene.

RAPID RECALL Q: What type of dinosaur skeleton is shown on the movie poster for *Jurassic Park*?
A: Tyrannosaurus rex

ORDER UP! **A.** After 27 years, the South African government releases Nelson Mandela from prison.
B. The Nobel Peace Prize is awarded jointly to South Africa's F. W. De Klerk and Nelson Mandela.
A. (1990) B. (1993)

HIT PARADE **Sing** a line from Shania Twain's 1997 crossover single "You're Still the One."

DEAD OR ALIVE? Ferdinand Marcos
Dead. The ousted Filipino leader kicked the bucket in 1989.

BLAST FROM **THE PAST**

9

FACT OR PHOOEY? TLC's Lisa "Left Eye" Lopes "accidentally" torched the mansion of her boyfriend, pro-football player Andre Risen in 1994.
Fact.

HOT OR NOT? Mighty Morphin' Power Rangers
Hot. In 1993, kids across the country became enthralled with the adventures of six normal kids turned super heroes.

RAPID RECALL **Q:** What city is home to the Hard Rock Café's first location?
A: London, England

ORDER UP! **A.** President Clinton outlines the first balanced budget in 30 years.
B. *Pulp Fiction* shows audiences Quentin Tarantino's explosive version of the L.A. underworld, and inspires a cult following.
B. (1994) A. (1998)

HIT PARADE **Q:** What pop diva had a "Vision of Love"—and a hit single—in 1990?
A: Mariah Carey

DEAD OR ALIVE? Lucille Ball
Dead. Ball died in 1989, but we can still love her in syndication seven days a week.

BLAST FROM THE PAST

10

FACT OR PHOOEY? First aired in 1991, *Where in the World is Carmen Sandiego?*, regularly featured the rock group Rockapella.
Fact.

HOT OR NOT? *Scary Movie*
Not. The horror genre did come back from the dead to rule the box office in the '90s, but this successful slasher spoof wasn't released until 2000.

RAPID RECALL **Q:** In *Babe*, how does farmer Hoggett come to own his prize-winning pig?
A: He wins him in a contest by guessing the pig's weight.

ORDER UP! **A.** Mike Tyson bites off part of Evander Holyfield's ear in a title fight.
B. Paul Reubens (a.k.a. Pee-Wee Herman) is arrested in a Florida movie theater for indecent exposure.
A. (1997) B. (1991)

HIT PARADE **Q:** What couldn't Gunnar and Matthew Nelson live without in 1990?
A: "Your Love and Affection"

DEAD OR ALIVE? Carroll O'Connor
Alive. TV's Archie Bunker didn't pass away until 2001.

BLAST FROM **THE PAST**

11

FACT OR PHOOEY? Actress Drew Barrymore has her own film production company called Phone Home Films.
Phooey! Barrymore's production company is called Flower Films.

HOT OR NOT? Baby On Board Signs
Not. Created in 1985 as a safety measure, Baby On Board signs were pretty much history by the '90s.

RAPID RECALL **Q:** What actress/singer played Selena in the 1997 movie about the Tejano pop sensation's short life?
A: Jennifer Lopez

ORDER UP! **A.** Renee Zellweger creates her break-out performance as a single mom in the Tom Cruise vehicle *Jerry Maguire*.
B. Gay college student Matthew Shepard is fatally beaten in Laramie, Wyoming.
A. (1996) B. (1998)

HIT PARADE **Q:** What 1990s one-hit wonder group thought they were too sexy for their shirts?
A: Right Said Fred ("I'm Too Sexy")

DEAD OR ALIVE? E. B. White
Dead. The *Charlotte's Web* author bought the farm in 1985.

BLAST FROM THE PAST

12

FACT OR PHOOEY? In *Dances with Wolves,* the Sioux tribe befriends Kevin Costner's character, Lt. John Dunbar.
Fact.

HOT OR NOT? Boy Bands
Hot. From New Kids to Backstreet to *NSync, the '90s were bookended by boys. The names and faces may have morphed, but the fans stayed true.

RAPID RECALL **Q:** What 1999 low-budget hit was filmed with a hand-held camera and had a bewitching effect on audiences around the globe?
A: *The Blair Witch Project*

ORDER UP! **A.** East and West Germany are reunited.
B. Mother Teresa dies in Calcutta at age 87.
A. (1990) B. (1997)

HIT PARADE **Q:** What is the title of the song Elton John rewrote as a tribute to Princess Diana in 1997 after her death?
A: "Candle in the Wind"

DEAD OR ALIVE? HRH Princess Margaret (British royal)
Alive. Her Majesty the Queen's sister lived royally until 2002.

BLAST FROM THE _PAST_

13

FACT OR PHOOEY? In _Romy & Michelle's High School Reunion_, Lisa Kudrow's character tells her classmates that she invented Wite-Out®.
Phooey! Kudrow claimed to be the inventor of the Post-it note.

HOT OR NOT? The _X-Men_ movie
Not. The comic book universe of the X-men was created in 1963 and didn't mutate to the big screen until 2000.

RAPID RECALL **Q:** What is the title of the controversial _Gone with the Wind_ sequel, released in 1991?
A: _Scarlett_

ORDER UP! **A.** Tina Brown steps down as editor of _The New Yorker_.
B. _ER_ and _Friends_ debut on NBC, establishing NBC's dominance of the Thursday-night lineup.
B. (1994) A. (1998)

HIT PARADE **Q:** Name the '80s supergroup that had a '90s hit with "Ordinary World."
A: Duran Duran

DEAD OR ALIVE? Anthony Quinn
Alive. With more than 100 motion pictures under his belt, this _Zorba the Greek_ actor lived until 2001.

BLAST FROM THE PAST

14

FACT OR PHOOEY?   *Lois & Clark* actress Teri Hatcher went on to star as Sally in a road tour of the musical *Cabaret*.
Fact.

HOT OR NOT?   Coffee Bars
Hot. Starbucks expanded from 84 locations in 1990 to 2,135 by 1999. "Getting coffee" replaced dinner and a movie in dating vocabulary.

RAPID RECALL   **Q:** What cunning forest animal has the same name as Mulder on *The X-Files*?
A: Fox

ORDER UP!   **A.** A terrorist's truck bomb blows up the block-long Oklahoma City Federal Building, killing 168 people.
B. The world awaits the consequences of the Y2K bug.
A. (1995) B. (1999)

HIT PARADE   **Q:** What is the name of Christina Aguilera's magical first hit, released in 1999?
A: "Genie in a Bottle"

DEAD OR ALIVE?   Alec Guinness (actor)
Alive. The *Star Wars* and *The Bridge on the River Kwai* actor passed away in 2000.

BLAST FROM **THE** PAST

15

FACT OR PHOOEY? Singer Joan Osborne founded the Lilith Fair, a music festival featuring an all-female line-up.
Phooey! Osborne performed in the fair, but Sarah McLachlan started the festival in 1997.

HOT OR NOT? Debbie Gibson
Not. Gibson topped the charts in the late '80s, but by the '90s, not even reinventing herself as Deborah could get her back on the charts.

RAPID RECALL Q: In what country was the comfortable and trendy Birkenstock footwear created?
A: Germany

ORDER UP! A. John Grisham's novel *The Firm* becomes a runaway best seller.
B. Clinton appoints Madeleine Albright as the first female U.S. Secretary of State.
A. (1991) B. (1996)

HIT PARADE **Sing** a line from the Spice Girls' first single, "Wannabe," released in the U.S. in 1997, **or** tell which "Spice" Emma Bunton is?
A: Baby Spice

DEAD OR ALIVE? Danny Kaye (actor)
Dead. This unique comic actor and star of *The Secret Life of Walter Mitty* died in 1987.

16

FACT OR PHOOEY? In 1997, Pacific Gas & Electric's CEO Gordon Smith banned from its employee newsletter what comic strip that takes a cynical look at office-life?
Fact. *Dilbert*

HOT OR NOT? *The Rugrats*
Hot. One of the three original NickToons, *Rugrats'* tots took the '90s by storm, becoming the longest running original program in the network's history.

RAPID RECALL **Q:** What Anne Rice novel was made into a 1994 movie starring Tom Cruise?
A: *Interview with a Vampire*

ORDER UP! **A.** George Burns dies at 100.
B. The number of Internet users worldwide reaches 150 million. Over 50% are from the United States.
A. (1996) B. (1999)

HIT PARADE **Sing** a line from Eric Clapton's 1992 tribute to his late son.
A: "Tears in Heaven"

DEAD OR ALIVE? Richard Burton
Dead. Liz's legendary love died in 1984.

17

FACT OR PHOOEY?   Matthew Broderick was the adult voice of Simba in the 1994 movie *The Lion King.*
Fact.

HOT OR NOT?   The iMac
Hot. Introduced in 1998, Apple's colorful, unpack, plug-in, and turn-on personal computer revolutionized the industry and flew off store shelves.

RAPID RECALL   **Q:** How many *Free Willy* movies were released in the 1990s?
A: Three (*Free Willy, Free Willy 2: The Adventure Home, Free Willy 3: The Rescue*)

ORDER UP!   **A.** Terrorists bomb U.S. embassies in Kenya and Tanzania.
B. Steven Spielberg wins his first directing Oscar® for *Schindler's List.*
B. (1994) A. (1998)

HIT PARADE   **Q:** What pop star made baldness a little more beautiful when her 1990 release, "Nothing Compares 2 U" hit the Top 40?
A: Sinead O'Connor

DEAD OR ALIVE?   John Lee Hooker
Alive. This Blues icon didn't bid the world adieu till 2001.

BLAST FROM THE PAST

18

FACT OR PHOOEY? In the 1990 release *Misery,* Kathy Bates' character, Annie Wilkes, kidnaps author Paul Sheldon because she thinks he's a bad writer.
Phooey! Wilkes claims to be Sheldon's "Number One Fan."

HOT OR NOT? The Coreys—Haim and Feldman
Not. The actors and teen pinups found themselves plagued by direct-to-video films by the end of the '80s.

RAPID RECALL Q: What restaurant sprung up in cities across the U.S. as a direct result of the movie *Forrest Gump*?
A: Bubba Gump Shrimp Co.

ORDER UP! A. Israeli Prime Minister Yitzhak Rabin is slain by a Jewish extremist at a peace rally.
B. Millions tune in to watch Barbara Walters sit down with Monica Lewinsky in her first televised interview.
A. (1995) B. (1999)

HIT PARADE Q: What musical icon wanted to know if you could be "The Most Beautiful Girl in the World" in a 1994 single?
A: Prince

DEAD OR ALIVE? Salvador Dali (artist)
Dead. The Spanish surrealist said goodbye in 1989.

BLAST FROM THE PAST

19

FACT OR PHOOEY? On *Xena: Warrior Princess*, the royal one's loyal sidekick is a dwarf named Gene.
Phooey! Xena's trusty—and gutsy—companion is Gabrielle.

HOT OR NOT? *The People's Court* with Judge Wapner
Not. Judge Wapner held court for twelve years, but a whole new breed of judges, led by the no-holds-barred Judge Judy, took TV by storm in the '90s.

RAPID RECALL **Q:** Jerry Seinfeld's former girlfriend, Shoshana Lonstein, capitalized on her newfound fame with her own line of what in 1998?
A: Lingerie

ORDER UP! **A.** Viagra sells for a record $10.00 per tablet.
B. Bill Clinton is elected President, with Al Gore as Vice President; the Democrats keep control of Congress.
B. (1992) A. (1998)

HIT PARADE **Q:** According to his 1999 hit, what kind of life was Ricky Martin living?
A: "La Vida Loca"

DEAD OR ALIVE? Walter Matthau (actor)
Alive. The Oscar®-winning actor didn't pass away until 2000.

BLAST FROM THE PAST

20

FACT OR PHOOEY? Dylan McDermott, star of ABC's *The Practice*, met his wife, actress Shiva Rose, while filming a court scene for the TV drama.
Phooey! The two met in an L.A. café.

HOT OR NOT? MTV's Rock the Vote
Hot. MTV's aggressive voter awareness campaign and national bus tour helped increase young voter turnout in the '90s.

RAPID RECALL **Q:** In 1993, Anna Paquin became the youngest person to win an Academy Award® for her role in what movie?
A: *The Piano*

ORDER UP! **A.** River Phoenix dies of a drug overdose on Halloween at the age of 23.
B. Ellen DeGeneres outs herself, and becomes the first openly gay woman to have her own sitcom.
A. (1993) B. (1997)

HIT PARADE **Q:** What Patti Smith song did 10,000 Maniacs bring back to the charts in 1994?
A: "Because the Night"

DEAD OR ALIVE? Bette Davis
Dead. Hollywood's legendary leading actress turned up her toes in 1989.

BLAST FROM THE PAST

21

FACT OR PHOOEY? *Chicken Skin* is a popular Saturday morning TV show based on a series of books by R. L. Stine.
Phooey! The hit show, which first aired in 1995, was called *Goosebumps*.

HOT OR NOT? Beanie Babies
Hot. These cuddly offspring of stuffed animals and beanbag chairs captivated kids and collectors in the 1990s.

RAPID RECALL **Q:** Model/actress Vickie Lynn Hogan was criticized for marrying an aging oil tycoon in 1994. What name does Vickie answer to today?
A: Anna Nicole Smith

ORDER UP! **A.** Janet Jackson signs an $80 million deal with Virgin Records, making her the highest paid musician in history.
B. Olympic figure skater Nancy Kerrigan is brutally attacked.
B. (1994) A. (1996)

HIT PARADE **Sing** a line from Beck's "Loser."

DEAD OR ALIVE? Timothy McVeigh
Alive. McVeigh didn't meet his maker till 2001.

BLAST FROM THE PAST

22

FACT OR PHOOEY? Talk show host Oprah Winfrey boosted the 1996 Tickle Me Elmo craze when she gave the doll to audience members.
Phooey! Rosie O'Donnell was the gal who gave the Sesame Street doll a sales push.

HOT OR NOT? Elian Gonzalez
Not. The controversial plight of the young Cuban boy and his family made headlines, but not until 2000.

RAPID RECALL **Q:** What horror trilogy did *Party of Five*'s Neve Campbell star in?
A: *Scream*

ORDER UP! **A.** A Los Angeles jury finds O. J. Simpson not guilty of murder charges.
B. The Gulf War is broadcast live on TV.
B. (1991) A. (1995)

HIT PARADE **Q:** What legendary guitarist with a rotating back-up band reemerged in 1999 with an album that was "*Supernatural*"?
A: Carlos Santana

DEAD OR ALIVE? John Belushi
Dead. The *Saturday Night Live* regular OD'd at age 33 in 1982.

23

FACT OR PHOOEY? In 1992, vice president Dan Quayle criticized TV character Murphy Brown for having a child out of wedlock.
Fact.

HOT OR NOT? Drew Barrymore
Hot. The child actress found herself back in the spotlight in the '90s with movies like *The Wedding Singer* and *Ever After*.

RAPID RECALL **Q:** What *Cheers* spin-off debuted in 1993 and features a neurotic psychiatrist living in Seattle?
A: *Frasier*

ORDER UP! **A.** The lead singer of the grunge rock band Nirvana, Kurt Cobain, kills himself at age 27.
B. 77-year-old Senator John Glenn, the first American to orbit the earth, returns to orbit in the space shuttle *Discovery*.
A. (1994) B. (1998)

HIT PARADE **Q:** Name the two of the three 1990s Aerosmith videos that feature Alicia Silverstone.
A: "Crying," "Amazing," "Crazy"

DEAD OR ALIVE? Charles Schulz (*Peanuts* creator)
Alive. Schulz didn't retire Charlie Brown and the gang until weeks before his death in 2000.

24

FACT OR PHOOEY? The 1991 movie *Fried Green Tomatoes* is based on a 1959 Broadway musical.
Phooey! It's based on a 1987 Fannie Flagg novel.

HOT OR NOT? Anti-apartheid rallies
Not. The need to rally against the South African system faded along with the system itself in the early '90s.

RAPID RECALL Q: Which *South Park* character is seriously injured in every episode: Cartman, Chef, or Kenny?
A: Kenny

ORDER UP! A. *American Beauty* blossoms at the box office.
B. A car bomb explodes in New York's World Trade Center.
B. (1993) A. (1999)

HIT PARADE Q: What did the band Kris Kross make listeners want to do in 1992?
A: Jump

DEAD OR ALIVE? Tom Landry (Dallas Cowboys coach)
Alive. The long time Cowboys coach died in 2000 at age 75.

BLAST FROM
THE PAST

25

FACT OR PHOOEY? A Tamagotchi is the name for a computerized pet that needs attention to stay alive.
Fact. Released in 1997, these electronic pets thrilled obsessive-compulsive tykes, and traumatized the rest.

HOT OR NOT? *Survivor*
Not. The ratings grabbing trials of 16 regular people thrust into the wilderness didn't banish the competition until the summer of 2000.

RAPID RECALL **Q:** In what animated 1999 movie did Barbie make her movie debut?
A: *Toy Story 2*

ORDER UP! **A.** Compact discs surpass cassette tapes as the preferred medium for recorded music.
B. Nations pledge $1.23 billion in aid to rebuild Bosnia.
A. (1992) B. (1996)

HIT PARADE **Q:** What was the bum's name in a 1993 Arrested Development song?
A: Mr. Wendel

DEAD OR ALIVE? George Harrison
Alive. The "quiet" Beatle died in 2001 after a long fight against cancer.

26

FACT OR PHOOEY? Hillary Rodham Clinton's 1996 bestseller was titled *To Raise a Child*.
Phooey! Clinton's book, *It Takes A Village*, is named from the beginning
of the popular phrase, not the end.

HOT OR NOT? Dennis Rodman
Hot. Known as much for his off-court antics as for his game, Rodman
kept himself firmly in the spotlight until his retirement in 1999.

RAPID RECALL **Q:** What hallucination of Ally McBeal's became an email-
forwarding favorite after airing on the TV series in the '90s?
A: A dancing baby

ORDER UP! **A.** Gopher, the first user-friendly Internet interface, is created at
the University of Minnesota and named after the school mascot.
B. U.S. attorneys allege that Microsoft tried to control access to
the Internet.
A. (1991) B. (1998)

HIT PARADE **Q:** Fill in the blanks from this 1999 Barenaked Ladies' hit:
"Chickity China the Chinese _____/ You have a drumstick and
your brain stops _____."
A: Chicken; tickin' (from "One Week")

DEAD OR ALIVE? Lillian Hellman
Dead. Hollywood's once blacklisted writer passed away in 1984.

BLAST FROM THE PAST

27

FACT OR PHOOEY?   Released in 1999, Sega's Sonic is a warthog.
Phooey! Sonic is a hedgehog.

HOT OR NOT?   *Small Wonder*
Not. The syndicated adventures of Vickie the robot ran out of energy by 1989.

RAPID RECALL   **Q:** What 1998 Farrelly Brothers movie features Matt Dillion as sleazy P.I. Pat Healy?
A: *There's Something About Mary*

ORDER UP!   **A.** Brooklyn police are charged with the brutal beating of Haitian Abner Louima.
B. *Jurassic Park* hits pay dirt as the highest-grossing movie of all time.
B. (1993) A. (1997)

HIT PARADE   **Q:** What Orange County, California band broke into the Top 40 with their 1995 release *Tragic Kingdom*?
A: No Doubt

DEAD OR ALIVE?   Hank Ketchum (*Dennis the Menace* cartoonist)
Alive. Ketchum didn't call it quits till 2001.

BLAST FROM THE PAST

28

FACT OR PHOOEY? *Bill Nye the Science Guy* debuted in 1993 to critical fanfare, but never won an Emmy.
Phooey! The show (and guy) that made science fun for kids received over a dozen Emmys by the end of the decade.

HOT OR NOT? Pogs
Hot. Created in the 1920s, it took 70 years for this game in which players try to flip discs with a slammer to gain widespread popularity.

RAPID RECALL **Q:** In 1992, which version of Elvis did Americans chose for a postage stamp: the younger or older Elvis?
A: The younger Elvis

ORDER UP! **A.** After 30 years in late night, Johnny Carson hosts *The Tonight Show* for the last time.
B. Jonathan Larson's musical *Rent* wins the Pulitzer Prize for drama and the Tony for best musical.
A. (1992) B. (1996)

HIT PARADE **Q:** What 1995 animated film featured the Oscar®- and Grammy®-winning song, "Colors of the Wind"?
A: *Pocahontas*

DEAD OR ALIVE? Ray Bolger (*The Wizard of Oz*'s Scarecrow)
Dead. Bolger was buried in 1987.

BLAST FROM THE PAST

29

FACT OR PHOOEY? In *Mad About You*, characters Paul and Jamie first meet at a Manhattan newsstand.
Fact.

HOT OR NOT? Jenny McCarthy
Hot. The former Playboy model's popularity soared after landing a role on MTV's GenX dating show *Singled Out*.

RAPID RECALL **Q:** How many Oscars® did *The Silence of the Lambs* take home?
A: Four (Best Picture, Director, Actress, Actor)

ORDER UP! **A.** Clinton wins the Presidency, and is the first Democrat reelected since FDR.
B. Tennis legend Arthur Ashe announces that he contracted AIDS from a blood transfusion.
B. (1992) A. (1996)

HIT PARADE **Sing** a line from Michael Jackson's "Black or White."

DEAD OR ALIVE? Georgia O'Keeffe
Dead. The famous painter died at 98 years old in 1986.

BLAST FROM THE PAST

30

FACT OR PHOOEY? The Brady Act, signed in 1993, imposes a waiting period for gun possession and ownership.
Fact.

HOT OR NOT? Baseball record breakers
Hot. In the '90s, Cal Ripken Jr. played games 2,131 through 2,632, and Mark McGwire and Sammy Sosa chased each other for the homerun record.

RAPID RECALL Q: Which actress played teenager Amy Fischer in the TV special authorized by the Butafuccos?
A: Alyssa Milano (Drew Barrymore played the teen in the unauthorized version.)

ORDER UP! A. Director Stanley Kubrick dies at his home outside London.
B. Hi-tech "smart" bombs have 90% accuracy in the Gulf War.
B. (1991) A. (1999)

HIT PARADE Q: What red-headed country rocker had a 1992 hit with "I Can't Make You Love Me"?
A: Bonnie Raitt

DEAD OR ALIVE? Liberace
Dead. This flamboyant pianist, born Wladziu Valentino Liberace, died in 1986.

BLAST FROM THE PAST

31

FACT OR PHOOEY? Following its big screen debut in 1994, *Ace Ventura: Pet Detective* was made into a cartoon series, with Jim Carrey voicing the title role. Phooey! The movie did go animated, but Michael Hall gave Ace his voice on the small screen.

HOT OR NOT? Fluorescent clothing. Not. The days of day-glo dressing were blessedly a part of the past by the '90s.

RAPID RECALL **Q:** Redux and what other waist-shrinking drug got yanked from the market by the FDA in the 1990s? A: Fen-phen

ORDER UP! **A.** The Communist Party relinquishes sole power in the Soviet government. **B.** Tom Hanks wins his second consecutive Oscar® for Best Actor, for his role in *Forrest Gump*. A. (1990) B. (1994)

HIT PARADE **Q:** What 1994 release made Lisa Loeb the first unsigned artist to have a number one single? "Stay (I Missed You)" (from the *Reality Bites* soundtrack)

DEAD OR ALIVE? Ken Kesey Alive. The author of *One Flew Over the Cuckoo's Nest* didn't die till 2001.

BLAST FROM THE PAST

32

FACT OR PHOOEY? The character Audrey on TV's *Ellen*, which first aired in 1995, is always seen wearing the color blue.
Phooey! Audrey, played by Clea Lewis, only felt pretty in pink.

HOT OR NOT? Dilbert
Hot. The myopic and much put-upon engineer of Scott Adams's comic strip decorated '90s cubicles nation-wide.

RAPID RECALL **Q:** Name two of the main female characters, excluding adults, in the original season of the hit high school soap *Beverly Hills 90210*.
A: Brenda Walsh, Kelly Taylor, Donna Martin, or Andrea Zuckerman

ORDER UP! **A.** *Star Wars: Episode I: The Phantom Menace* opens and breaks a string of box-office records.
B. Heaven's Gate cult members commit mass suicide, hoping to reach a "spaceship" on the Hale-Bopp Comet.
B. (1997) A. (1999)

HIT PARADE **Q:** You oughta know . . . What former Canadian pop princess hit the U.S. with an anthem for angry young women in 1995?
A: Alanis Morissette

DEAD OR ALIVE? Ingrid Bergman (actress)
Dead. *Casablanca's* Ilsa Lund Lazlo died in 1982.

BLAST FROM **THE PAST**

33

FACT OR PHOOEY? Members of the quartet Boyz II Men met in high school.
Fact. They met at the Philadelphia High School of Creative and Performing Arts.

HOT OR NOT? The Titanic
Hot. The allure of the "unsinkable" ship's tragic fate got a boost from James Cameron's 1997 blockbuster movie.

RAPID RECALL Q: What charming star played Kimberly, the oldest Brock sibling, on the television series *Picket Fences*?
A: Holly Marie Combs

ORDER UP! **A.** *ER*'s George Clooney bids farewell to Chicago's Cook County General Hospital.
B. The U.S. sends food and troops to aid famine relief in war-torn Somalia.
B. (1992) A. (1999)

HIT PARADE **Sing** a line from the Green Day hit "When I Come Around" or name the 1994 album on which it was featured.
A: *Dookie*

DEAD OR ALIVE? Waylon Jennings
Alive. Country's legendary musician kept on crooning until 2002.

BLAST FROM THE PAST

34

FACT OR PHOOEY? The beginning of the romantic comedy *Sleepless In Seattle* is set during the Christmas holiday season.
Fact.

HOT OR NOT? Napster controversy
Not. The controversial software appeared in 1999, but it took a year for record execs and users to publicly clash over free downloads.

RAPID RECALL **Q:** Is Ren, of *Ren and Stimpy*, a cat, a dog, or a mouse?
A: A dog

ORDER UP! **A.** The Queen of England publicly urges Charles to divorce Diana.
B. President George Bush (senior) is briefly hospitalized for a heart irregularity.
B. (1991) A. (1995)

HIT PARADE **Q:** What *CrazySexyCool* trio warned, "Don't go chasing waterfalls" in 1994?
A: TLC

DEAD OR ALIVE? Louis L'Amour (author)
Dead. The author of many novels about the Old West died in 1988.

BLAST FROM THE *PAST*

35

FACT OR PHOOEY? *Being John Malkovich* director Spike Jonze married Steven Spielberg's oldest daughter in 1999.
Phooey! Jonze got hitched to Sofia Coppola (daughter of Francis Ford) in 1999.

HOT OR NOT? Garfield cats on windows
Not. For most drivers, Garfield was a goner by the 1990s.

RAPID RECALL **Q:** What kind of creature is Pikachu?
A: A Pokémon

ORDER UP! **A.** The White House launches a Web page and the first Internet commerce sites are established.
B. Baseball great Mark McGwire hits a record 70 home runs.
A. (1994) B. (1998)

HIT PARADE **Sing** a line from the 1995 hit "No More 'I Love You's' " or name the ex-Eurythmic who sang it.
A: Annie Lenox

DEAD OR ALIVE? Bill Haley (musician)
Dead. The *Rock Around the Clock* musician died in 1981.

BLAST FROM THE PAST

36

FACT OR PHOOEY? Keri Russell starred as *Dawson's Creek*'s Joey in the show's first season in 1998 before she landed the lead in *Felicity*.
Phooey! Katie Holmes is the original Joey.

HOT OR NOT? Barney
Hot. The big purple dinosaur enthralled preschoolers and drove parents batty in the '90s.

RAPID RECALL **Q:** What German import was favored in the "car wrapping" advertising craze during the dot-com boom?
A: Volkswagon Bug

ORDER UP! **A.** Aussie Mel Gibson plays a courageous warrior who does it all for love in *Braveheart*.
B. Reverend Jerry Falwell outs Tinky Winky, the purple Teletubby with a purse.
A. (1995) B. (1999)

HIT PARADE **Sing** a line from the Dave Matthews Band hit "What Would You Say."

DEAD OR ALIVE? Rita Hayworth
Dead. Hollywood's glamour girl died in 1987.

BLAST FROM **THE** PAST

37

FACT OR PHOOEY?   Waldo, of the *Where's Waldo* series, sports a striped shirt and ski cap.
Fact.

HOT OR NOT?   *Friday Night Videos*
Not. As more and more homes got cable and MTV, the late-night network countdown became little more than an infomercial alternative for insomniacs.

RAPID RECALL   **Q:** In the cult classic *Pulp Fiction*, what American equivalent do Jules and Vincent say Parisians call "royales"?
A: The Quarter Pounder

ORDER UP!   **A.** Women win all five gold medals collected by the U.S at the Albertville Winter Olympic Games.
B. Actor Billy Bob Thornton receives high praise for his role as a mentally challenged murderer in *Sling Blade*.
A. (1992) B. (1996)

HIT PARADE   **Sing** a line of the 1970s Roberta Flack song that The Fugees took to the top of the charts in 1996.
A: "Killing Me Softly With His Song"

DEAD OR ALIVE?   Ray Walston (actor)
Alive. Everybody's favorite Martian lived into 2001.

BLAST FROM THE PAST

38

FACT OR PHOOEY?   Writer Alan Ball won the 1999 best original screenplay Oscar® for *The Usual Suspects*.
Phooey! Ball won in 1999 for *American Beauty*.

HOT OR NOT?   Cell phones
Hot. Once just an inconvenient status symbol of the wealthy, dropping prices put cell phones into the hands of millions.

RAPID RECALL   **Q:** Which diva's dance album began a cowboy fashion trend in the late '90s?
A: Madonna (*Music*)

ORDER UP!   **A.** After 13 seasons and countless cliffhangers, the nighttime soap *Dallas* ends.
B. Former singer Sonny Bono, known best for being half of "Sonny and Cher," becomes a U.S. congressman.
A. (1991) B. (1995)

HIT PARADE   **Q:** What band did Jon Secada sing backup for before embarking on a solo career?
A: The Miami Sound Machine

DEAD OR ALIVE?   Peggy Lee (singer)
Alive. The woman who brought us "Fever" in the '50s lived till 2002.

39

FACT OR PHOOEY? Former Brat Packer Andrew McCarthy played Bill Gates in the 1999 made-for TV movie, *Pirates of Silicon Valley.*
Phooey! Anthony Michael Hall portrayed the billionaire.

HOT OR NOT? Beavis and Butthead
Hot. The crude, and crudely animated, adventures of these two high school slackers made them the anti-heroes of MTV.

RAPID RECALL Q: What cultural icon and tribute includes over 37,000 panels and covers over 16 acres?
A: The AIDS Quilt

ORDER UP! A. The first live online Internet birth occurs.
B. E. Annie Proulx's *The Shipping News,* a quiet tale of rebirth, wins the Pulitzer Prize and the National Book Award.
B. (1994) A. (1998)

HIT PARADE Q: What classic Beatles' tune was the theme song for the early '90s hit show, *Life Goes On*?
A: "Ob-La-Di, Ob-La-Da"

DEAD OR ALIVE? Roy Orbison (singer)
Dead. The "Only the Lonely" and "Crying" singer died in 1988.

BLAST FROM THE PAST

40

FACT OR PHOOEY? "Something Funny Is Happening in L.A." was the movie tagline for 1997's *L.A. Confidential.*
Phooey! It was for *L.A. Story,* released in 1991.

HOT OR NOT? Pee-Wee Herman
Not. The Paul Reubens persona of films and Saturday morning TV was put to rest after his 1991 arrest for indecent exposure.

RAPID RECALL **Q:** Which actor did supermodel Cindy Crawford star alongside in the 1995 box-office bomb *Fair Game*?
A: William Baldwin

ORDER UP! **A.** Hong Kong returns to Chinese rule.
B. *Chicago Tribune* film critic Gene Siskel, of Siskel and Ebert fame, dies at age 53.
A. (1997) B. (1999)

HIT PARADE **Q:** Bruce Springsteen had two major hits in the '90s with movie themes for *Philadelphia* and *Jerry Maguire.* Name one of the two song titles.
A: "Streets of Philadelphia" or "Secret Garden"

DEAD OR ALIVE? Nancy Marchand (actress)
Alive. Tony's mother on *The Sopranos* kept on kicking till 2000.

41

FACT OR PHOOEY? Billy Bob Thornton won the best original screenplay Oscar® in 1997 for a movie he also starred in and directed.
Fact. Thornton took home a little gold man for *Sling Blade*.

HOT OR NOT? Ankle-zipper Jeans
Not. Introduced by Guess? in the early '80s, ankle zippers on skin-tight jeans gave way to relaxed fits and boot cuts.

RAPID RECALL **Q:** Who was the first African American author to win the Nobel Prize for Literature?
A: Toni Morrison (in 1993)

ORDER UP! **A.** Israel elects Benjamin Netanyahu as prime minister.
B. HBO's series *Sex and the City* takes a revealing and comedic look at the New York dating scene.
A. (1996) B. (1998)

HIT PARADE **Q:** Name the band that released the 1992 dance track, "Rhythm is a Dancer."
A: Snap!

DEAD OR ALIVE? Steve Allen (talk show host)
Alive. *The Tonight Show*'s original host didn't give his final curtain call until 2000.

BLAST FROM THE PAST

42

FACT OR PHOOEY? *Politically Incorrect*'s Bill Maher never went to college, opting instead to go on a comedy road tour that launched his career.
Phooey! Maher has a degree in English from Cornell University.

HOT OR NOT? *The Brady Bunch*
Hot. This '70s hit came back in a big way with two big screen movies that transplanted America's favorite blended family into the '90s.

RAPID RECALL **Q:** Name the doctor of psychology who became an *Oprah Winfrey* regular in 1998.
A: Dr. Phil (McGraw)

ORDER UP! **A.** Woodstock II kicks off in upstate New York.
B. Jay Leno succeeds Johnny Carson as the host of *The Tonight Show*.
B. (1991) A. (1999)

HIT PARADE **Q:** Name two of Britney Spears' three 1999 Top 10 singles.
A: "Baby, One More Time," "(You Drive Me) Crazy," "Sometimes"

DEAD OR ALIVE? Hugh Beaumont (*Leave it to Beaver*'s Ward Cleaver)
Dead. The Beave's dad died in 1982.

BLAST FROM THE PAST

43

FACT OR PHOOEY?   In 1991, Pamela Anderson became *Home Improvement*'s very first "Tool Time Girl."
Fact.

HOT OR NOT?   "Don't Worry, Be Happy"
Not. Bobby McFerrin's blockbuster song hit the charts in 1988.

RAPID RECALL   Q: What '90s sci-fi TV cult fave featured movie commentary from both humans and robots—and is known as "MST3K"?
A: *Mystery Science Theater 3000*

ORDER UP!   **A.** America's "Dream Team" of NBA all-stars clobbers the competition and slam-dunks the gold at the Barcelona Olympics.
B. Two boys, aged 11 and 12, shoot four of their schoolmates in Jonesboro, Arkansas.
A. (1992) B. (1998)

HIT PARADE   **Sing** a line from Aerosmith's 1998 number one single, "I Don't Wanna Miss A Thing."

DEAD OR ALIVE?   William Hanna
Alive. Yabba-dabba do! This half of the Hanna-Barbera team lived until 2001.

BLAST FROM THE PAST

44

FACT OR PHOOEY? According to an episode in the show's second season (1993–94), a *Melrose Place* apartment rented for $1,000 a month.
Phooey! *The Melrose Place* pads went for $800 a month.

HOT OR NOT? Political scandals
Hot. The '90s saw investigations, resignations and a near presidential impeachment.

RAPID RECALL Q: According to the best-selling book, what type of soup is good for the soul?
A: *Chicken Soup*

ORDER UP! A. The Prince of Pop is born to Michael Jackson and wife Debbie Rowe.
B. The Rock and Roll Hall of Fame Museum opens in Cleveland, Ohio.
B. (1995) A. (1997)

HIT PARADE Q: In 1997, Aqua sang about being what kind of girl?
A: Barbie (from "Barbie Girl")

DEAD OR ALIVE? Chuck Jones (cartoonist)
Alive. The creator of Bugs Bunny, Daffy Duck, and Wile E. Coyote didn't say "That's All Folks!" until 2002.

BLAST FROM THE PAST

45

FACT OR PHOOEY? At one point in his life, '90s cult leader David Koresh spent several years in Los Angeles trying to become a rock star.
Fact.

HOT OR NOT? Jem
Not. Glam-girl and rocker Jem may have starred in her own cartoon but in the long run she couldn't compete with Barbie.

RAPID RECALL **Q:** In what five-star hotel does little Kevin McCallister reside during *Home Alone II: Lost in New York*?
A: The Plaza Hotel

ORDER UP! **A.** Russia fights to avert financial collapse.
B. Professional baseball player Pete Rose is sentenced to five months for income tax evasion.
B. (1990) A. (1998)

HIT PARADE **Q:** What R&B star ushered the single "You Make Me Wanna . . ." on to the charts?
A: Usher

DEAD OR ALIVE? Ansel Adams
Dead. The landscape photographer known for his black and white images died in 1984.

BLAST FROM THE PAST

46

FACT OR PHOOEY? The grunge look started as part of an underground music movement in Berkeley, California.
Phooey! The grunge movement got its roots in Seattle.

HOT OR NOT? New Wave
Not. New Wave was old news; besides, the look was too high maintenance for '90s slackers to handle.

RAPID RECALL **Q:** What renowned reference book series takes a humorous approach to how-to?
A: The "For Dummies" series

ORDER UP! **A.** Nicholas Cage plays a drunk who falls for a hooker with a heart of gold in *Leaving Las Vegas*.
B. The Soviet Union breaks up after President Gorbachev's resignation.
B. (1991) A. (1995)

HIT PARADE **Q:** No one was crying for Madonna when she had a hit from what 1996 movie soundtrack?
A: *Evita*

DEAD OR ALIVE? Jason Robards (actor)
Alive. The Oscar®-winning actor lived until 2000.

BLAST FROM THE PAST

47

FACT OR PHOOEY? Rodney King won a settlement against the city of Los Angeles in a civil law suit for $3.8 million.
Fact.

HOT OR NOT? The Spice Girls
Hot. These prefab femmes hit the scene with a call for girl power and got it with astronomical albums and ticket sales.

RAPID RECALL **Q:** What kind of animal is *Blue's Clues* Blue?
A: A dog

ORDER UP! **A.** A pipe bomb explodes at the Olympic Games in Atlanta, Georgia.
B. Gennifer Flowers alleges a long-time affair with presidential candidate Bill Clinton.
B. (1992) A. (1996)

HIT PARADE **Q:** Name the funky divas that sang these lyrics in a 1992 single: "Never never gonna get it (no not this time),/no you're never gonna get it (my love) . . ."
A: En Vogue (from "My Lovin' (Never Gonna Get It))" on *Funky Divas*

DEAD OR ALIVE? Victor Borge (pianist)
Alive. The "funniest pianist on Earth" tickled the keys till his death in 2000.

BLAST FROM THE PAST

48

FACT OR PHOOEY?   The production numbers for the 1995 Las Vegas movie *Showgirls* were actually filmed in a Lake Tahoe hotel.
Fact.

HOT OR NOT?   Gangsta' Rap
Hot. The gritty truth of life in the inner city started gaining ground in the late '80s and continued to find a voice with artists like Snoop Dogg and Biggie Smalls.

RAPID RECALL   **Q:** After their excellent adventure, what kind of journey did Bill and Ted take in 1991?
A: A bogus journey (in *Bill and Ted's Bogus Journey*)

ORDER UP!   **A.** Tara Lipinski beats fellow American figure skater Michelle Kwan for the gold medal at the Olympics.
B. A policy of "Don't ask, don't tell" is adopted by the U.S. military to deal with gay people in the ranks.
B. (1993) A. (1998)

HIT PARADE   **Q:** What rapper released *The Slim Shady LP* in 1999?
A: Eminem (a.k.a. Marshall Mathers)

DEAD OR ALIVE?   Cary Grant (actor)
Dead. Born Archie Leach, this *Arsenic and Old Lace* actor passed away in 1986.

BLAST FROM **THE** PAST

49

FACT OR PHOOEY?   Actor Mel Gibson played Shakespeare's Henry V in a 1990 box office production.
Phooey! Mel Gibson played Shakespeare's Hamlet, not his Henry.

HOT OR NOT?   Papal apologies
Not. Pope John Paul II made an unprecedented apology for wrongs perpetrated by the church, but he didn't do so until March of 2000.

RAPID RECALL   **Q:** What color is the Teletubby Po?
A: Red

ORDER UP!   **A.** In her divorce settlement, Princess Di gets $26 million but loses the title "Royal Highness."
B. The FDA approves the Flavr Savr tomato, the first genetically engineered food product.
A. (1996) B. (1994)

HIT PARADE   **Q:** What pint-sized pop star had a hit with "Rush" in 1991?
A: Paula Abdul

DEAD OR ALIVE?   Perry Como
Alive. *Catch a Falling Star*'s crooner croaked in 2001.

BLAST FROM THE *PAST*

50

FACT OR PHOOEY? Julia Robert's first Oscar® nomination was for her role in 1990's *Pretty Woman*.
Phooey! She received the Oscar nod for her role in *Steel Magnolias*, released a year earlier.

HOT OR NOT? *Seinfeld*
Hot. The show about nothing gave the public something it was looking for and was a ratings sensation in the '90s.

RAPID RECALL **Q:** What annoying (but lovable!) dork did Jaleel White play on *Family Matters*?
A: Urkel

ORDER UP! **A.** The first McDonald's opens in Moscow.
B. Hillary Clinton is named chair of the Health Reform Task Force.
A. (1990) B. (1993)

HIT PARADE **Q:** What band hit it big with the 1992 ballad "To Be with You"?
A: Mr. Big

DEAD OR ALIVE? Jackie Gleason (actor)
Dead. *The Honeymooners'* Ralph Kramden died in 1987.

BLAST FROM
THE PAST

51

FACT OR PHOOEY? Texas had the most championship teams in major pro sports (baseball, basketball, hockey, and football) during the 1990s.
Fact.

HOT OR NOT? Dotcom IPOs
Hot. In the '90s, Internet companies with questionable ideas and a URL went public and made mega bucks—on paper.

RAPID RECALL Q: What 1997 novel follows the life of a young slave girl in the Gion district of Kyoto?
A: *Memoirs of a Geisha*

ORDER UP! A. The controversial television ratings system debuts on cable stations and broadcast networks.
B. Grateful Dead front man and renowned hippie guitarist Jerry Garcia dies.
B. (1995) A. (1997)

HIT PARADE Q: Woodstock II was in 1994. In what year was the original Woodstock?
A: 1969

DEAD OR ALIVE? Yul Brynner (actor)
Dead. The Russian-born *The King and I* star died in 1985.

BLAST FROM THE PAST

52

FACT OR PHOOEY?   Michael Jordan retired from retirement by re-signing with the Chicago Bulls in 1995.
Fact.

HOT OR NOT?   Rush Limbaugh
Hot. Love him or hate him, the conservative radio show host developed a legion of loyal fans that became known as "Dittoes" in the '90s.

RAPID RECALL   Q: What is the name of the "stuttering" Howard Stern staff member?
A: Stuttering John

ORDER UP!   **A.** Republicans nominate Bob Dole and Jack Kemp to take on the incumbent Clinton-Gore ticket.
B. During the Lillehammer games, the women's figure skating final becomes the sixth highest-rated broadcast of any sort in U.S. television history.
B. (1994) A. (1996)

HIT PARADE   Sing a line from *Nsync's "Tearin' Up My Heart."

DEAD OR ALIVE?   Phil Silvers (comedian/actor)
Dead. Sergeant Bilko died in 1985.

53

FACT OR PHOOEY? In 1992, Vice President Dan Quayle mistakenly corrected a 6th grader's spelling of the word tomato.
Phooey. Quayle coached the 6th grader to add an "e" to the word "potato."

HOT OR NOT? *Twin Peaks*
Hot. Devoted fans tuned into this '90s phenomenon produced by David Lynch and Mark Frost.

RAPID RECALL **Q:** What kind of animal is Dolly, who was made famous in 1997 for her cloned genes?
A: A sheep

ORDER UP! **A.** The FDA approves use of the surgically-implanted contraceptive Norplant.
B. The Menendez brothers go on trial for the murder of their parents.
A. (1990) B. (1993)

HIT PARADE **Q:** What famed photographer directed Janet Jackson's 1990 "Love Will Never Do (Without You)" video?
A: Herb Ritts

DEAD OR ALIVE? Tito Puente (composer and bandleader)
Alive. The "Mambo King" played on till 2000.

BLAST FROM THE PAST

54

FACT OR PHOOEY?   Former Philippine first lady Imelda Marcos went on trial in 1990 for fronting a black market ring that sold designer shoes.
Phooey! Mrs. Marcos' 1990 trial was for money-laundering, not a shoe ring fraud.

HOT OR NOT?   Jams
Not. It was the surf culture of the '80s (not the '90s) that inspired these oversized attention-grabbing shorts.

RAPID RECALL   Q: Christie's held an auction in 1997 for what pop-culture icon's collection of gowns?
A: Diana, Princess of Wales

ORDER UP!   **A.** The Sojourner vehicle roams Mars and sends back pictures.
B. Elizabeth Taylor marries her eighth husband, 39-year-old carpenter Larry Fortensky.
A. (1997) B. (1991)

HIT PARADE   Q: What country singer had a crossover hit with "This Kiss" in 1998?
A: Faith Hill

DEAD OR ALIVE?   Spike Milligan (comedian)
Alive. The "godfather of British comedy" kept 'em laughing until 2002.

BLAST FROM **THE** **PAST**

55

FACT OR PHOOEY? NC-17 was implemented as a new movie rating in the 1990s.
Fact.

HOT OR NOT? Million Man March
Hot. Louis Farrakhan organized this 1995 march on Washington that called on African American men to work to rebuild their communities.

RAPID RECALL **Q:** Which drug did Elizabeth Wurtzel refer to in the title of her 1996 book about a young woman struggling with depression?
A: Prozac (in *Prozac Nation*)

ORDER UP! **A.** Woody Allen and Mia Farrow go to court over custody of their three children.
B. Major league baseball players go on strike.
A. (1992) B. (1994)

HIT PARADE **Q:** What 1998 Semisonic hit included the line "You don't have to go home, but you can't stay here"?
A: "Closing Time"

DEAD OR ALIVE? Gilda Radner
Dead. The much-loved and talented *Saturday Night Live* actress died in 1989.

BLAST FROM THE PAST

56

FACT OR PHOOEY? Despite its namesake, the first Planet Hollywood was opened in New York.
Phooey! The restaurant's first location was in Orange County, California.

HOT OR NOT? Furby
Hot. These teachable toys invaded homes everywhere in the '90s.

RAPID RECALL **Q:** Who plays Matt Damon's love interest in 1997's *Good Will Hunting*?
A: Minnie Driver

ORDER UP! **A.** Legendary crooner Frank Sinatra dies of a heart attack at age 82.
B. President George Bush signs the Clean Air Act.
A. (1998) B. (1990)

HIT PARADE **Sing** a line from the Ally McBeal theme song "Searching My Soul" or name its singer.
A: Vonda Shepard

DEAD OR ALIVE? Les Brown (musician)
Alive. The man whose band's big hit was "Sentimental Journey" (with Doris Day on vocals) died in 2001.

BLAST FROM THE *PAST*

57

FACT OR PHOOEY? Gymnast Mary Lou Retton was voted one of the top ten faces for the 1999 Wheaties 75th Anniversary cereal package.
Fact.

HOT OR NOT? Harry Potter
Hot. J. K. Rowling worked literary wizardry with her series that had kids and adults alike lining up for reading material.

RAPID RECALL Q: Tyra Banks sported a mustache for which 1990s ad campaign?
A: Got Milk?

ORDER UP! A. 25-year-old rapper Tupac Shakur is shot and killed in a drive-by shooting.
B. Baseball player Cal Ripkin of the Baltimore Orioles sets a record for having played 2,131 consecutive games in the major leagues.
B. (1995) A. (1996)

HIT PARADE Q: What former Stray Cat hit it big with a remake of the classic "Jump, Jive, An' Wail"?
A: Brian Setzer

DEAD OR ALIVE? Hedy Lamarr
Alive. The *Boom Town* actress, once referred to as the "World's Most Beautiful Woman," died in 2000.